# AI ENHANCED CYBER THREATS

**Dr. R. Shalini**
Associate Professor,
Dept of CSE, Sathyabama Institute
of Science and Technology

**Dr. K. Veena**
Associate Professor,
Dept of CSE, Sathyabama Institute
of Science and Technology

KHANNA BOOK
PUBLISHING CO. (P) Ltd.
4C/4344, Ansari Road, Darya Ganj,
New Delhi, India

Sathyabama Institute of
Science and Technology
Jeppiaar Nagar, Rajiv Gandhi Salai,
Chennai, Tamilnadu, India

Dear Readers,

To prevent the piracy, this book is secured with HIGH SECURITY HOLOGRAM on the front title cover. In case you don't find the hologram on the front cover title, please write us to at contact@khannabooks.com or whatsapp us at +91-99109 09320 and avail special gift voucher for yourself.

Specimen of Hologram on front Cover title:

Moreover, there is a SPECIAL DISCOUNT COUPON for you with EVERY HOLOGRAM.

How to avail this SPECIAL DISCOUNT:

Step 1: Scratch the hologram
Step 2: Under the scratch area, your "coupon code" is available
Step 3: Logon to www.khannabooks.com
Step 4: Use your "coupon code" in the shopping cart and get your copy at a special discount
Step 5: Enjoy your reading!

Thanks,
Khanna Publishing House

**ISBN:** 978-93-55388-24-7

**AI Enhanced Cyber Threats**
*by* **Dr. R. Shalini, Dr. K. Veena**

**First Edition:** 2025

To view complete list of books, please scan the QR Code:

*Published by:*
**Khanna Book Publishing Co. (P) Ltd.**
CIN: U22110DL1998PTC095547

Visit us at: www.khannabooks.com
Write us at: contact@khannabooks.com

Printed in Bharat.

# Preface

The rise of artificial intelligence (AI) has brought about transformative advancements across industries, from healthcare and finance to automation and cybersecurity. However, alongside its benefits, AI has also introduced new and more sophisticated cyber threats. Cybercriminals, nation-state actors, and malicious organizations are now leveraging AI-driven tools to enhance their attack strategies, evade detection, and exploit vulnerabilities in ways that were once unimaginable. This book explores the dark side of AI in cybersecurity, shedding light on how intelligent algorithms are being weaponized to carry out cyberattacks with unprecedented efficiency and scale.AI-enhanced cyber threats are evolving rapidly, making traditional security measures increasingly ineffective. From deepfake-driven social engineering attacks to AI-powered malware that adapts to countermeasures, the threat landscape is becoming more dynamic and unpredictable.

Automated phishing campaigns, adversarial AI techniques, and autonomous hacking systems now enable cybercriminals to bypass security protocols, manipulate digital identities, and disrupt critical infrastructure. As AI continues to improve, the sophistication of these attacks will only increase, posing significant risks to individuals, businesses, and governments worldwide.This book delves into the mechanics of AI-driven cyber threats, analyzing real-world incidents, emerging trends, and potential future risks. It discusses how attackers exploit machine learning models, deceive AI-powered security systems, and manipulate large datasets to carry out cyber espionage, fraud, and sabotage. By raising awareness and fostering discussions on responsible AI usage, we can work towards securing the digital world against the next generation of intelligent cyber threats.

# Contents

◆◆◆

# 1 UNIT

# Introduction and Problem Solving

## 1.1 INTRODUCTION

### Acting Humanly: The Turing Test Approach

- The Turing Test, proposed by Alan Turing TURING TEST (1950), was designed to provide a satisfactory operational definition of intelligence.
- A computer passes the test if a human interrogator, after posing some written questions, cannot tell whether the written responses come from a person or from a computer. For now, we note that programming a computer to pass a rigorously applied test provides plenty to work on. The computer would need to possess the following capabilities:

### Acting Humanly: The Turing Test Approach

- Natural language processing to enable it to communicate successfully in English;
- Knowledge representation to store what it knows or hears;
- Automated reasoning to use the stored information to answer questions and to draw
- Machine learning to adapt to new circumstances and to detect and extrapolate patterns.
- To pass the total Turing Test, the computer will need
- Computer vision to perceive objects, and
- Robotics to manipulate objects and move about.

## 1.2 UNDERSTANDING AI BASICS

a. Psychology is the scientific study of the mind and behavior. Psychologists are actively involved in studying and understanding mental processes, brain functions, and behavior.

b. Cognitive psychology is the branch of psychology dedicated to studying how people think. The cognitive perspective in psychology focuses on how the interactions of thinking, emotion, creativity, and problem-solving abilities affect how and why you think the way you do.

c. Decision theory (or the theory of choice; not to be confused with choice theory is a branch of applied probability theory and analytic philosophy concerned with the theory of making decisions based on assigning probabilities to various factors and assigning numerical consequences to the outcome.

d. Neuroscience is the study of the nervous system – from structure to function, development to degeneration, in health and in disease. It covers the whole nervous system, with a primary focus on the brain. Incredibly complex, our brains define who we are and what we do.

## 1.3 HISTORY OF AI

a. The gestation of artificial intelligence (1943–1955)
b. The birth of artificial intelligence (1956)
c. Early enthusiasm, great expectations (1952–1969)
d. A dose of reality (1966–1973)
e. Knowledge-based systems: The key to power? (1969–1979)
f. AI becomes an industry (1980–present)
g. The return of neural networks (1986–present)
h. AI adopts the scientific method (1987–present)
i. The emergence of intelligent agents (1995–present)
j. The availability of very large data sets (2001–present)

## 1.4 INTELLIGENT AGENTS AND THEIR ROLE IN SECURITY

An intelligent agent is a program that can make decisions or perform a service based on its environment, user input and experiences. These programs can be used to autonomously gather information on a regular, programmed schedule or when prompted by the user in real time. An intelligent agent is also referred to as a bot, which is short for robot.

Typically, an agent program, using parameters the user has provided, searches all or some part of the internet, gathers information the user is interested in, and presents it to them on a periodic or requested basis. Data intelligent agents can extract any specifiable information, such as keywords or publication date.

Agents that use artificial intelligence (AI) and machine learning use sensors, such as microphones and cameras, to collect user input. They also use effectors, such as fingers and wheels, to affect their environment, as well as actuators, such as speakers and screens, to deliver agent output. The practice of having information brought to a user by an agent is called push notification technology.

Rational Agent: A rational agent is an agent which has clear preference, models uncertainty, and acts in a way to maximize its performance measure with all possible actions.

For each possible percept sequence, a rational agent should select an action that is expected to maximize its performance measure, given the evidence provided by the percept sequence and whatever built-in knowledge the agent has.

What is rational at any given time depends on four things:

- The performance measure that defines the criterion of success.
- The agent's prior knowledge of the environment.

- The actions that the agent can perform.
- The agent's percept sequence to date.

## Specifying the Task Environment

- Fully observable vs. partially observable
- Single agent vs. multiagent
- Deterministic vs. stochastic
- Episodic vs. sequential:
- Static vs. dynamic:
- Discrete vs. continuous
- Known vs. unknown

Deterministic vs. stochastic. If the next state of the environment is completely determined by the current state and the action executed by the agent, then we say the environment is deterministic; otherwise, it is stochastic.

We say an UNCERTAIN environment is uncertain if it is not fully observable or not deterministic.

NONDETERMINISTIC environment is one in which actions are characterized by their possible outcomes, but no probabilities are attached to them. Nondeterministic environment descriptions are usually associated with performance measures that require the agent to succeed for all possible outcomes of its actions.

Episodic vs. sequential: In an episodic task environment, the agent's experience is SEQUENTIAL divided into atomic episodes. In each episode the agent receives a percept and then performs a single action. Crucially, the next episode does not depend on the actions taken in previous episodes. Many classification tasks are episodic.

Static vs. dynamic: If the environment can change while an agent is deliberating, then we say the environment is dynamic for that agent; otherwise, it is static. Static environments are easy to deal with because the agent need not keep looking at the world while it is deciding on an action, nor need it worry about the passage of time. Dynamic environments, on the other hand, are continuously asking the agent what it wants to do; if it hasn't decided yet, that counts as deciding to do nothing. If the environment itself does not change with the passage of time but the agent's performance score does, then we say the environment is semidynamic.

Discrete vs. continuous: The discrete/continuous distinction applies to the state of the CONTINUOUS environment, to the way time is handled, and to the percepts and actions of the agent. For example, the chess environment has a finite number of distinct states (excluding the clock). Chess also has a discrete set of percepts and actions. Taxi driving is a continuous-state and continuous-time problem:

Known vs. unknown: Strictly speaking, this distinction refers not to the environment UNKNOWN itself but to the agent's (or designer's) state of knowledge about the "laws of physics" of the environment. In a known environment, the outcomes (or outcome probabilities if the environment is stochastic) for all actions are given. Obviously, if the environment is unknown, the agent will have to learn how it works in order to make good decisions.

### Structure And Types of agents

1. Simple reflex agents
2. Model-based reflex agents
3. Goal-based agents
4. Utility-based agent

**Agent programs**

agent = architecture + program

## 1.5 PROBLEM SOLVING AGENTS

In artificial intelligence, a problem-solving agent refers to a type of intelligent agent designed to address and solve complex problems or tasks in its environment. These agents are a fundamental concept in AI and are used in various applications, from game-playing algorithms to robotics and decision-making systems.

### Goal Formulation

Imagine an agent in the city of Arad, Romania, enjoying a touring holiday. The agent's performance measure contains many factors: it wants to improve its suntan, improve its Romanian,take in the sights, enjoy the nightlife (such as it is), avoid hangovers, and so on. The decision problem is a complex one involving many trade offs and careful reading of guidebooks.Now, suppose the agent has a non refundable ticket to fly out of Bucharest the following day. In that case, it makes sense for the agent to adopt the goal of getting to Bucharest. Courses of action that don't reach Bucharest on time can be rejected without further consideration and the agent's decision problem is greatly simplified. Goals help organize behaviour by limiting the objectives that the agent is trying to achieve and hence the actions it needs to consider. Goal formulation, based on the current situation and the agent's performance measure, is thefirst step in problem solving.

Problem formulation is the process of deciding what actions and states to consider, given a goal.Our agent has now adopted the goal of driving to Bucharest and is considering where to go from Arad.Three roads lead out of Arad, one toward Sibiu, one to Timisoara, and one to Zerind.achieves the goal, so unless the agent is familiar with the geography of Romania, it will not know whichroad to follow. In other words, the agent will not know which of its possible actions is best, because it does not yet know enough about the state that results from taking each action. We assume that the environment is observable, so the agent always knows the current state. For the agent driving in Romania, it's reasonable to suppose that each city on the map has a sign indicating itspresence to arriving drivers.

We also assume the environment is discrete, so at any given state there are only finitely many actions to choose from.This is true for navigating in Romania because each city is connected to a small number of othercities.We will assume the environment is known, so the agent knows which states are reached by eachaction.Finally, we assume that the environment is deterministic, so each action has exactly one outcome.

### Toy Problems

The first example we examine is the vacuum world first introduced in this can be formulated as a problem as follows:

- **States:** The state is determined by both the agent location and the dirt locations. The agent is in one of two locations, each of which might or might not contain dirt. Thus, there are 2 × 22 = 8 possible world states. A larger environment with n locations has n ▪ 2n states.
- **Initial state:** Any state can be designated as the initial state.
- **Actions:** In this simple environment, each state has just three actions: Left, Right, and Suck. Larger environments might also include Up and Down.
- **Transition model:** The actions have their expected effects, except that moving Left in the leftmost square, moving Right in the rightmost square, and Sucking in a clean square have no effect. The complete state space is shown in Figure 3.3.
- **Goal test:** This checks whether all the squares are clean.
- **Path cost:** Each step costs 1, so the path cost is the number of steps in the path.

## 8-Puzzle Problem

- **States:** A state description specifies the location of each of the eight tiles and the blank in one of the nine squares.
- **Initial state:** Any state can be designated as the initial state. Note that any given goal can be reached from exactly half of the possible initial states.
- **Actions:** The simplest formulation defines the actions as movements of the blank space Left, Right, Up, or Down. Different subsets of these are possible depending on where the blank is.
- **Transition model:** Given a state and action, this returns the resulting state; for example, if we apply Left to the start state in Figure 3.4, the resulting state has the 5 and the blank switched.
- **Goal test:** This checks whether the state matches the goal configuration shown in Figure
- (Other goal configurations are possible.)
- **Path cost:** Each step costs 1, so the path cost is the number of steps in the path.

What abstractions have we included here? The actions are abstracted to their beginning

## 8-Queens Problem

- States: Any arrangement of 0 to 8 queens on the board is a state.
- Initial state: No queens on the board.
- Actions: Add a queen to any empty square.
- Transition model: Returns the board with a queen added to the specified square.
- Goal test: 8 queens are on the board, none attacked.

## Real-world Problems

a. Route-finding problem
b. Touring problems
c. traveling salesperson problem
d. VLSI layout

e. Robot navigation
f. Automatic assembly sequencing

A search problem consists of:

- A State Space. Set of all possible states where you can be.
- A Start State. The state from where the search begins.
- A Goal State. A function that looks at the current state returns whether or not it is the goal state.

The Solution to a search problem is a sequence of actions, called the plan that transforms the start state to the goal state.

## 1.6. UNINFORMED SEARCH STRATEGIES

This section covers several search strategies that come under the heading of uninformed search (also called blind search). The term means that the strategies have no additional UNINFORMED SEARCH BLIND SEARCH information about states beyond that provided in the problem definition. All they can do is generate successors and distinguish a goal state from a non-goal state. All search strategies are distinguished by the order in which nodes are expanded. Strategies that know whether INFORMED SEARCH one non- goal state is "more promising" than another are called informed search or heuristic

### Heuristic Search (Search Strategies)

1. Breadth-first search
2. Uniform-cost search
3. Depth-first search
4. Depth-limited search
5. Iterative deepening depth-first search

Breadth-first search https://www.geeksforgeeks.org/breadth-first-search-or-bfs-for-a-graph

The Breadth First Search (BFS) algorithm is used to search a graph data structure for a node that meets a set of criteria. It starts at the root of the graph and visits all nodes at the current depth level before moving on to the nodes at the next depth level.

## 1.7 SEARCHING WITH PARTIAL INFORMATION (INFORMED HEURISTICS SEARCH STRATEGIES)

BEST-FIRST SEARCH The general approach we consider is called best-first search. Best-first search is an instance of the general TREE-SEARCH or GRAPH-SEARCH algorithm in which a node is selected for expansion based on an evaluation function, f(n). The evaluation function is EVALUATION FUNCTION construed as a cost estimate, so the node with the lowest evaluation is expanded first. The implementation of best-first graph search is identical to that for uniform-cost search (Figure 3.14), except for the use of f instead of g to order the priority queue. The choice of f determines the search strategy. (For example, as Exercise 3.21 shows, best-first tree search includes depth-first search as a special case.) Most best-first algorithms include as a component of f a heuristic function, denoted h(n): HEURISTIC FUNCTION h(n) = estimated cost of the cheapest path from the state at node n to a goal state. (Notice that h(n) takes a node as input, but, unlike g(n), it depends only on the state at that node.) For example, in Romania, one might estimate the cost of the cheapest path from Arad to Bucharest via the straight-line distance from Arad to Bucharest. Heuristic functions are the most common form in which additional knowledge of the problem is imparted to the search algorithm. For now, we consider them to be arbitrary, nonnegative, problem-specific functions, with one constraint: if n is a goal node, then h(n)=0. The remainder of this section covers two ways to use heuristic information to guide search.

1. Greedy best-first search
2. A* search: Minimizing the total estimated solution cost
3. Memory-bounded heuristic search
4. Learning to search better

## Greedy Best-First Search

https://www.geeksforgeeks.org/greedy-best-first-search-algorithm/ Greedy Best-First Search is an AI search algorithm that attempts to find the most promising path from a given starting point to a goal. It prioritizes paths that appear to be the most promising, regardless of whether or not they are actually the shortest path. The algorithm works by evaluating the cost of each possible path and then expanding the path with the lowest cost. This process is repeated until the goal is reached.

The algorithm works by using a heuristic function to determine which path is the most promising. The heuristic function takes into account the cost of the current path and the estimated cost of the remaining paths. If the cost of the current path is lower than the estimated cost of the remaining paths, then the current path is chosen. This process is repeated until the goal is reached.

## How Greedy Best-First Search Works?

- Greedy Best-First Search works by evaluating the cost of each possible path and then expanding the path with the lowest cost. This process is repeated until the goal is reached.
- The algorithm uses a heuristic function to determine which path is the most promising.
- The heuristic function takes into account the cost of the current path and the estimated cost of the remaining paths.
- If the cost of the current path is lower than the estimated cost of the remaining paths, then the current path is chosen. This process is repeated until the goal is reached.

An example of the best-first search algorithm is below graph, suppose we have to find the path from A to G

1. We are starting from A, so from A there are direct path to node B (with heuristics value of 32), from A to C (with heuristics value of 25) and from A to D (with heuristics value of 35).
2. So as per best first search algorithm choose the path with lowest heuristics value, currently C has lowest value among above node . So we will go from A to C.
3. Now from C we have direct paths as C to F ( with heuristics value of 17) and C to E (with heuristics value of 19), so we will go from C to F.

4. Now from F we have direct path to go to the goal node G (with heuristics value of 0), so we will go from F to G.
5. So now the goal node G has been reached and the path we will follow is A → C → F → G

## Advantages of Greedy Best-First Search

1. **Simple and Easy to Implement:** Greedy Best-First Search is a relatively straightforward algorithm, making it easy to implement.
2. **Fast and Efficient:** Greedy Best-First Search is a very fast algorithm, making it ideal for applications where speed is essential.
3. **Low Memory Requirements:** Greedy Best-First Search requires only a small amount of memory, making it suitable for applications with limited memory.
4. **Flexible:** Greedy Best-First Search can be adapted to different types of problems and can be easily extended to more complex problems.
5. **Efficiency:** If the heuristic function used in Greedy Best-First Search is good to estimate, how close a node is to the solution, this algorithm can be a very efficient and find a solution quickly, even in large search spaces.

## Disadvantages of Greedy Best-First Search

1. **Inaccurate Results:** Greedy Best-First Search is not always guaranteed to find the optimal solution, as it is only concerned with finding the most promising path.
2. **Local Optima:** Greedy Best-First Search can get stuck in local optima, meaning that the path chosen may not be the best possible path.
3. **Heuristic Function:** Greedy Best-First Search requires a heuristic function in order to work, which adds complexity to the algorithm.
4. **Lack of Completeness:** Greedy Best-First Search is not a complete algorithm, meaning it may not always find a solution if one is exists. This can happen if the algorithm gets stuck in a cycle or if the search space is a too much complex.

## Applications of Greedy Best-First Search

1. **Pathfinding:** Greedy Best-First Search is used to find the shortest path between two points in a graph. It is used in many applications such as video games, robotics, and navigation systems.
2. **Machine Learning:** Greedy Best-First Search can be used in machine learning algorithms to find the most promising path through a search space.
3. **Optimization:** Greedy Best-First Search can be used to optimize the parameters of a system in order to achieve the desired result.
4. **Game AI:** Greedy Best-First Search can be used in game AI to evaluate potential moves and chose the best one.
5. **Navigation:** Greedy Best-First Search can be use to navigate to find the shortest path between two locations.
6. **Natural Language Processing:** Greedy Best-First Search can be use in natural language processing tasks such as language translation or speech recognisation to generate the most likely sequence of words.

7. **Image Processing:** Greedy Best-First Search can be use in image processing to segment image into regions of interest.

## 1.8 FUNDAMENTALS OF AI FOR SECURITY

AI security is a key component of enterprise cybersecurity that focuses on defending AI infrastructure from cyberattacks. Focusing on AI security is vital because numerous AI technologies are woven into the fabric of organizations. AI is the engine behind modern development processes, workload automation, and big data analytics. It's also increasingly becoming an integral component of many products and services. For example, a banking app provides financial services, but AI-powered technologies like chat bots and virtual assistants within these apps provide an X factor.

### AI Security Risks

The best way to tackle AI security is to thoroughly understand the risks. Let's take a look at the biggest AI security risks.

The integration of AI, such as Gen AI, into SDLCs fundamentally changes an enterprise's IT infrastructure and introduces many unknown risks. This is essentially a broadening of the attack surface. The overarching security challenge of AI is to ensure that all AI infrastructure is under the stewardship of security teams. Complete visibility of AI infrastructure can help remediate vulnerabilities, reduce risks, and limit your attack surface.

AI pipelines tend to broaden the vulnerability spectrum. For instance, the realm of data science, encompassing data and model engineering, often operates beyond traditional application development boundaries, leading to novel security risks.

The process of gathering, processing, and storing data is fundamental in the domain of machine learning engineering. Integrating with model engineering tasks demands robust security protocols to protect data from breaches, intellectual property theft, supply chain attacks, and data manipulation or poisoning. Ensuring data integrity is pivotal in reducing both deliberate and accidental data discrepancies.

### Data poisoning

Data poisoning is the manipulation of Gen AI models. It involves inputting malicious datasets to influence outcomes and create biases. The Trojan Puzzle, an attack designed by researchers, is an example of how threat actors might be able to influence and infect datasets that a Gen AI model learns from to choreograph malicious payloads.

### Direct Prompt Injections

Direct prompt injections are a type of attack where threat actors deliberately design LLM prompts intending to compromise or ex filtrate sensitive data. There are numerous risks associated with direct prompt injection, including malicious code execution and the exposure of sensitive data.

## 1.9 DEEP LEARNING FUNDAMENTALS FROM A SECURITY PERSPECTIVE

Deep learning algorithms use deep neural networks to "think" like a human brain and can adjust themselves to data properties they are trained on. That makes it easier for it to adapt automatically to the massive volume of threats out there.

Deep Learning is also called hierarchical learning and deep-structured learning, and it is comprised of supervised or unsupervised machine learning techniques. The idea of Deep Learning derived from the structure and functionality of the human brain and also the processing of signals through neurons in the human mind. Deep Learning is also taking the benefits of artificial neural networks, and it also consists of input, output, and many hidden layers. Each layer of Deep Learning relies upon the nonlinear response based on the data provided through the input layer. For the last few years, the Deep Learning technique has been mostly and widely used in the signal processing of voice recognition, graphic recognition, discovery of the thing, and so numerous other areas, such as the discovery of the medicine for diseases and enomics . Deep Learning developed a structure to deal with big data sets through a backpropagation algorithm to highlight in what way the device changes its core parameters that are being opted to calculate the representation in each rendering layer in the previous layer.

## Application of Deep Learning

1. Self-Driving Car
2. DL in Healthcare
3. DL in Voice Search
4. Automatic Machine Translation
5. Automatic Handwriting Generation

## Deep Learning Threats and Attacks

Deep learning faces various types of threats and attacks, and all famous threats and attacks are listed below.

### *Causative Attack*

In the causative attack used to decrease the performance and reliability of the training processes, the machine learning algorithm provided incorrect training data after modification in the labels of the samples that are not covered under the decision limit. Many researchers performed causative attacks on the images and revealed that it expressively decreases the performance of the training phase.

This means that the opponents have the ability to change the input of training data, which becomes the cause of changes in the parameters of the learning models during recycling, resulting in a substantial reduction in the presentation of jobs in succeeding taxonomy tasks.

### *Exploratory Attack*

The exploratory attacks basically do not influence on a training dataset. The key objective of the exploratory attacks is to get knowledge with respect to the learning algorithm as much as it can about the basic system. Model invasion attack, model extraction, and membership inference are the examples of the exploratory attacks.

In a security break viewpoint, threats to Deep Learning may be characterized into 3 groups:

**(1) Integrity Attack.** The integrity attack occurs and then the Deep Learning models failed to trace the negative cases when categorizing harmful samples. The output of the system will clearly show that the integrity of the learning machine has been compromised. Suppose, we used spam filter to stop unwanted/harm messages, and if the attacker sends a message that has unwanted/harm words then, the filter does not get it. The integrity attack is tested through exploratory testing.

(2) **Availability Attack.** The availability attack is the opposite of an integrity attack in which the Deep Learning models filtered out the legitimate cases during the categorization of the unwanted/harmful samples. The output of the system will clearly show that the availability of the learning machine has been compromised and it is no more available and hacked. The DoS attack is one of the examples of availability wherein legitimate cases failed to cross the filters and ultimately the system becomes compromised.

(3) **Privacy Violation Attack.** In the privacy violation attack, the attacker becomes successful to get the sensitive/confidential information of the system from both training and learning models. In terms of attack privacy, security threats for Deep Learning have further 02 categories.

### *Targeted Attack*

It is highly dangerous, and it directly decreases the performance of the classifier in a single specific sample or set of one of the samples.

### *Indiscriminate Attack*

An indiscriminate attack is the subtype of the poisoning attack. The attacker's key goals are to increase the general classification error. Further, the indiscriminate attack always chooses a random value from the training sample. It randomly fails the classifier.

## 1.10 CYBER SECURITY SPACE PROBLEM SOLUTION

### Cybersecurity in Space: Recent Scenario

Now, you might think that space is far removed from your daily life but most of the technologies and infrastructure we depend on are circling the planet. From telecommunications satellites and GPS to internet connectivity and weather tracking, technology in space is crucial for global communication and innovation. A cyber-attack on space infrastructure can have devastating effects on everyone on the ground.

Cybersecurity for space exploration is also important to maintain secure lines of communication, accurate navigation, and precise control. Space exploration is already a critical venture that requires certainty and stability to ensure the safety of astronauts, technicians, and more. This means that cybersecurity in space should be a priority concern.

One of the biggest space cybersecurity threats is hacking into spacecraft and satellites. Cybercriminals can easily take control of vital systems, manipulate controls, and steal confidential data. Jamming and spoofing methods are often used to disrupt or slow down the communication of data from satellites. The war in Ukraine saw the use of jamming and other cyberattacks on the Starlink SpaceX terminal. Military leaders have said that these tactics are common weapons.

A research paper from the University of Oxford has also stated that the threat of cyber-attacks has risen due to space systems becoming "increasingly interconnected and computationally complex." However, most space stations and infrastructure were built before there was a global focus on cybersecurity. This means that these systems are highly complex but also highly vulnerable to cyber-attacks.

## Two Biggest Telescopes were Hacked - a Challenge in Space Cybersecurity

On the 1st of August, the National Science Foundation's National Optical-Infrared Astronomy Research Laboratory - or NOIRLab - reported a cybersecurity incident that halted operations at its Gemini North Telescope in Hawaii and Gemini South Telescope in Chile. These attacks came just a few days before the NCSC issued its advisory to American space companies and research organizations about the threat of cyber-attacks and espionage.

Smaller telescopes on Cerro Tololo in Chile were also affected and the staff are still unsure about how the attacks took place. According to a statement by NOIRLab, the recovery process of the affected facilities and telescopes is still ongoing. The scientific community suffers every moment that operations are disrupted by cyber-attacks – not only with expenses but also due to the data being lost during downtime.

## Limited Resources and Bandwidth Constraints

Without the right funding and internet, most countries around the world are battling to stay ahead in the space race. These limited resources can lead to low or non-existent security measures in place.

## Vulnerabilities in Satellite Systems and Ground Infrastructure

Between the complex operations between space, ground, links, and users, there are several potential vulnerabilities to contend with when it comes to space and ground infrastructure. Cyber threats now also have a larger target with the growing interest from private and commercial organizations. A few of the potentially vulnerable areas in existing space cybersecurity include:

1. Software-defined radio compromise.
2. Insider threats.
3. Hacking ground systems to interact with satellites.
4. Using design and hardware development to imbed malicious features.
5. Communications hacking on TT&C systems through command link injections, replay attacks, or electronic attacks such as jamming and spoofing.
6. Software vulnerabilities.

## Potential Impact of Cyber-Attacks on Space Missions

Cyber-attacks on space infrastructure can include malware installation, ransomware attacks, and data or system breaches. All these attacks can disrupt communications, supply chains, national security, internet access, and global economies. Space missions affected by cyber- attacks can also lead to the injury or death of astronauts, the destruction of property, and the halting of progress in space exploration.

## Space in Cybersecurity

As the space race intensifies and nations rush to create new and innovative technologies to keep up, cybersecurity for space is also becoming a lucrative market. Smaller businesses can seize this opportunity to fill the demand for cybersecurity measures for space technology. Forbes has listed a few ways that smaller companies can amplify their brand in this rapidly expanding sector:

1. Innovate and develop space cybersecurity solutions.
2. Stay informed on industry trends and legislation.
3. Establish thought leadership.
4. Collaborate with educational institutions.
5. Participate in industry associations and events.
6. Diversify service offerings.
7. Create strategic alliances.
8. Establish your brand as a pioneer in the field.

## Cybersecurity Measures for Space Missions

Space systems can be vulnerable because of features like hardcoded credentials – which are used by ships, planes, and the military and can be accessed easily by hackers. This is why space missions need enhanced cybersecurity measures that ensure the safe transmission of data. Some of the cybersecurity measures that can be used include:

- **Secure Communication Protocols and Encryption Techniques:** Keeping communications between ground and space stations secure is a crucial element of space cybersecurity. The use of encrypting techniques will ensure a protected line of communication that can be vital for the safety of lives, data, and technology.
- **Authentication and Access Control Mechanisms:** Maintaining the right access controls will ensure that only authorized personnel have access to critical infrastructure. Using a zero-trust policy will go a long way to keeping the space system secure.
- **Intrusion Detection and Prevention Systems:** Cyber threats need to be identified, isolated, and mitigated by the infrastructure in place. Space missions need to employ active intrusion detection and threat intelligence to root out cyber-attacks before they can do any damage to the system.
- **Data Encryption and Protection Strategies:** Hackers will try to ex filtrate satellite data or manipulate data to deliver incorrect transmissions. With data encryption, communications are secure, and the data cannot be stolen, manipulated, or damaged.

◆◆◆

*Intentionally left blank!*

2

UNIT

# Fundamentals of Cybersecurity

## 2.1 CORE SECURITY PRINCIPLES

### Identity

In cybersecurity, "identity" refers to the unique characteristics and attributes associated with an entity, such as a user, system, device, or application, within a digital environment. Establishing and managing identities is a fundamental aspect of cybersecurity, as it forms the basis for access control, authentication, and authorization. Here are key aspects of identity in cybersecurity:

#### *User Identity*

In the context of cybersecurity, user identity often involves the identification and verification of individuals accessing digital systems or services. User identities are typically managed through the use of credentials such as usernames and passwords, biometrics, smart cards, or other authentication methods.

### Access Control

Identity is closely tied to access control, which is the process of determining what resources or information a particular identity is allowed to access.

### Authentication

Authentication is a critical component of cybersecurity, serving as the process of verifying the claimed identity of an entity, such as a user, system, or device, to ensure that it is legitimate and authorized to access certain resources or perform specific actions. The primary goal of authentication in cybersecurity is to prevent unauthorized access and protect sensitive information. Here are key aspects of authentication in cybersecurity.

### Confidentiality

Confidentiality is a fundamental concept in cybersecurity that involves protecting information from unauthorized access, disclosure, or exposure. The goal is to ensure that sensitive data remains private and accessible only to those individuals or systems with the proper authorization. Maintaining confidentiality is crucial for safeguarding sensitive information and preventing potential security breaches. Here are key aspects of confidentiality in cybersecurity:

### Data Encryption

Encryption is a primary technique used to maintain confidentiality. It involves converting plaintext data into cipher text using cryptographic algorithms. Encrypted data is only readable to those with the appropriate decryption key, providing a secure way to protect sensitive information.

### Access Controls

Access controls restrict access to data based on the principle of least privilege, ensuring that individuals or systems have only the necessary permissions to access specific information.

Role-based access control (RBAC) and other access management strategies help enforce confidentiality by limiting access to authorized entities.

### Network Security

Network security measures, such as firewalls and intrusion detection/prevention systems, contribute to confidentiality by controlling the flow of data and preventing unauthorized access to networked resources.

### Secure Communication Protocols

Using secure communication protocols, such as HTTPS for web traffic or VPNs for private network communication, helps protect the confidentiality of data during transmission. These protocols encrypt data in transit, preventing eavesdropping and interception by unauthorized parties.

### Data Classification

Data classification involves categorizing information based on its sensitivity and importance. By assigning different levels of classification, organizations can implement specific security controls to protect highly sensitive data more rigorously.

### Physical Security

Physical security measures, such as secure data centers and restricted access areas, contribute to confidentiality by preventing unauthorized physical access to servers, storage devices, and other critical infrastructure.

### Data Masking and Redaction

Data masking and redaction involve obscuring or removing sensitive information from documents, databases, or other sources, while still allowing authorized users to access the non- sensitive parts.

This is often applied to protect personally identifiable information (PII) or sensitive financial data.

### Data Leakage Prevention (DLP)

DLP solutions help prevent the unauthorized disclosure of sensitive information by monitoring and controlling data transfers within an organization. They can identify and block attempts to transmit sensitive data outside the organization's network.

### Secure Storage

Protecting data at rest is essential for maintaining confidentiality. Secure storage mechanisms, including encrypted file systems and databases, help safeguard data when it is stored on physical or digital media.

Confidentiality, when effectively implemented alongside other cybersecurity principles, ensures that sensitive information remains private and secure, reducing the risk of data breaches and unauthorized access.

### Privacy

Privacy involves your right to manage your personal information, and security is the protection of this information. Both are equally important aspects of cyber safety. You have privacy rights and should take measures to secure your personal information and data within the digital environment.

### Anonymity

Anonymity means not having a name or other identifying information associated with one's online activities - email, phone number, full name, and other identifying information. In other words, it is the ability to use the internet without revealing one's identity.

### Availability

This means that the information is available to authorized users when it is needed. As defined in FISMA, the term 'availability' means ensuring timely and reliable access to and use of information. The property that data or information is accessible and usable upon demand by an authorized person. 2. Timely, reliable access to data and information services for authorized users.

### Integrity

Integrity in cyber security refers to the methods of ensuring that data is accurate, real, and safeguarded from unauthorised user modification or destruction. Data integrity also refers to the accuracy and validity of data over its entire lifecycle.

## 2.2 EXPLORING CRYPTOGRAPHIC ALGORITHMS TOGETHER WITH MAJOR ATTACKS

A cryptographic algorithm is the mathematical equation used to scramble the plain text and make it unreadable. They are used for data encryption, authentication and digital signatures.

Cryptography is technique of securing information and communications through use of codes so that only those person for whom the information is intended can understand it and process it. Thus preventing unauthorized access to information. The prefix "crypt" means "hidden" and suffix "graphy" means "writing". In Cryptography the techniques which are use to protect information are obtained from mathematical concepts and a set of rule based calculations known as algorithms to convert messages in ways that make it hard to decode it. These algorithms are used for cryptographic key generation, digital signing, verification to protect data privacy, web browsing on internet and to protect confidential transactions such as credit card and debit card transactions.

Techniques used for Cryptography: In today's age of computers cryptography is often associated with the process where an ordinary plain text is converted to cipher text which is the text made such that intended receiver of the text can only decode it and hence this process is known as encryption. The process of conversion of cipher text to plain text this is known as decryption.

**Features of Cryptography are as follows:**

- **Confidentiality:** Information can only be accessed by the person for whom it is intended and no other person except him can access it.
- **Integrity:** Information cannot be modified in storage or transition between sender and intended receiver without any addition to information being detected.
- **Non-repudiation:** The creator/sender of information cannot deny his intention to send information at later stage.
- **Authentication:** The identities of sender and receiver are confirmed. As well as destination/origin of information is confirmed.

## Types of Cryptography

In general there are different types of cryptography:

- **Symmetric Key Cryptography:** It is an encryption system where the sender and receiver of message use a single common key to encrypt and decrypt messages. Symmetric Key Systems are faster and simpler but the problem is that sender and receiver have to somehow exchange key in a secure manner. The most popular symmetric key cryptography system are Data Encryption System(DES) and Advanced Encryption System(AES).
- **Hash Functions:** There is no usage of any key in this algorithm. A hash value with fixed length is calculated as per the plain text which makes it impossible for contents of plain text to be recovered. Many operating systems use hash functions to encrypt passwords.
- **Asymmetric Key Cryptography:** Under this system a pair of keys is used to encrypt and decrypt information. A receiver's public key is used for encryption and a receiver's private key is used for decryption. Public key and Private Key are different. Even if the public key is known by everyone the intended receiver can only decode it because he alone know his private key. The most popular asymmetric key cryptography algorithm is RSA algorithm.

## Applications of Cryptography

1. **Computer passwords:** Cryptography is widely utilized in computer security, particularly when creating and maintaining passwords. When a user logs in, their password is hashed and compared to the hash that was previously stored. Passwords are hashed and encrypted before being stored. In this technique, the passwords are encrypted so that even if a hacker gains access to the password database, they cannot read the passwords.
2. **Digital Currencies:** To safeguard transactions and prevent fraud, digital currencies like Bitcoin also use cryptography. Complex algorithms and cryptographic keys are used to safeguard transactions, making it nearly hard to tamper with or forge the transactions.

3. **Secure web browsing:** Online browsing security is provided by the use of cryptography, which shields users from eavesdropping and man-in-the-middle assaults. Public key cryptography is used by the Secure Sockets Layer (SSL) and Transport Layer Security (TLS) protocols to encrypt data sent between the web server and the client, establishing a secure channel for communication.
4. **Electronic signatures:** Electronic signatures serve as the digital equivalent of a handwritten signature and are used to sign documents. Digital signatures are created using cryptography and can be validated using public key cryptography. In many nations, electronic signatures are enforceable by law, and their use is expanding quickly.
5. **Authentication:** Cryptography is used for authentication in many different situations, such as when accessing a bank account, logging into a computer, or using a secure network. Cryptographic methods are employed by authentication protocols to confirm the user's identity and confirm that they have the required access rights to the resource.
6. **Cryptocurrencies:** Cryptography is heavily used by cryptocurrencies like Bitcoin and Ethereum to safeguard transactions, thwart fraud, and maintain the network's integrity. Complex algorithms and cryptographic keys are used to safeguard transactions, making it nearly hard to tamper with or forge the transactions.
7. **End-to-End Encryption:** End-to-end encryption is used to protect two-way communications like video conversations, instant messages, and email. Even if the message is encrypted, it assures that only the intended receivers can read the message. End-to-end encryption is widely used in communication apps like WhatsApp and Signal, and it provides a high level of security and privacy for users.

## Advantages

1. **Access Control:** Cryptography can be used for access control to ensure that only parties with the proper permissions have access to a resource. Only those with the correct decryption key can access the resource thanks to encryption.
2. **Secure Communication:** For secure online communication, cryptography is crucial. It offers secure mechanisms for transmitting private information like passwords, bank account numbers, and other sensitive data over the internet.
3. **Protection against attacks:** Cryptography aids in the defence against various types of assaults, including replay and man-in-the-middle attacks. It offers strategies for spotting and stopping these assaults.
4. **Compliance with legal requirements:** Cryptography can assist firms in meeting a variety of legal requirements, including data protection and privacy legislation.

## Symmetric-Key Algorithms

### *AES (Advanced Encryption Standard)*

- **Description:** A widely used symmetric-key encryption algorithm.
- **Attack:** Side-channel attacks, such as timing attacks or power analysis, can be a threat.

### *DES (Data Encryption Standard)*

- **Description:** An early symmetric-key algorithm, now considered insecure due to its short key length.
- **Attack:** Brute-force attacks are a significant threat due to the small key space.

### *Blowfish*

- **Description:** A symmetric-key block cipher designed for fast encryption and decryption.
- **Attack:** No major practical attacks have been discovered, but it has a relatively short key length.

## Asymmetric (Public-Key) Algorithms

### *RSA (Rivest-Shamir-Adleman)*

- **Description:** A widely used public-key algorithm for secure data transmission.
- **Attack:** Integer factorization attacks (e.g., using Shor's algorithm for quantum computers) pose a threat to RSA, especially with small key sizes.

### *Elliptic Curve Cryptography (ECC)*

- **Description:** A public-key algorithm based on the mathematics of elliptic curves.
- **Attack:** Elliptic Curve Factorization (ECF) attacks can be a threat, especially if the curves are not carefully selected.

## Hash Functions

### *SHA-2 (Secure Hash Algorithm 2):*

- **Description:** A family of cryptographic hash functions widely used for data integrity and digital signatures.
- **Attack:** Theoretical collision attacks are known, but practical collisions are not feasible.

### *MD5 (Message Digest Algorithm 5):*

- **Description:** An older hash function, now considered insecure due to vulnerabilities.
- **Attack:** Collision attacks (two different inputs producing the same hash) have been demonstrated.

## Attacks and Vulnerabilities

### *Cryptanalysis*

- **Description:** The study of techniques to break cryptographic systems.
- **Examples:** Differential Cryptanalysis, Linear Cryptanalysis.

### *Brute-force Attacks*

- **Description:** Trying all possible keys until the correct one is found.
- **Examples:** Trying all possible passwords to decrypt data.

### *Side-Channel Attacks*

- **Description:** Exploiting information leaked during the cryptographic process (e.g., timing, power consumption).
- **Examples:** Timing attacks, Power analysis attacks.

### *Quantum Attacks*

- **Description:** Exploiting quantum computing algorithms to break certain cryptographic schemes.
- **Examples:** Shor's algorithm for integer factorization, Grover's algorithm for symmetric key search.

## 2.3 EXPLORING HIGH-LEVEL SECURITY PROTOCOLS

In today's world, we transfer the data in bulk, and the security of this data is very important, so Internet security provides that feature i.e., protection of data. There are different types of protocol exist like routing, mail transfer, and remote communication protocol. But the Internet security protocol helps in the security and integrity of data over the internet. There are many protocols that exist that help in the security of data over the internet such as Secure Socket Layer (SSL), Transport Layer Security (TLS).

### SSL Protocol

1. SSL Protocol stands for Secure Sockets Layer protocol, which is an encryption-based Internet security protocol that protects confidentiality and integrity of data.
2. SSL is used to ensure the privacy and authenticity of data over the internet.
3. SSL is located between the application and transport layers.
4. At first, SSL contained security flaws and was quickly replaced by the first version of TLS that's why SSL is the predecessor of the modern TLS encryption.
5. TLS/SSL website has "HTTPS" in its URL rather than "HTTP".
6. SSL is divided into three sub-protocols: the Handshake Protocol, the Record Protocol, and the Alert Protocol.

### TLS Protocol

1. Same as SSL, TLS which stands for Transport Layer Security is widely used for the privacy and security of data over the internet.
2. TLS uses a pseudo-random algorithm to generate the master secret which is a key used for the encryption between the protocol client and protocol server.
3. TLS is basically used for encrypting communication between online servers like a web browser loading a web page in the online server.
4. TLS also has three sub-protocols the same as SSL protocol – Handshake Protocol, Record Protocol, and Alert Protocol.

### SHTTP

1. SHTTP stands for Secure Hyper Text Transfer Protocol, which is a collection of security measures like Establishing strong passwords, setting up a firewall, thinking of antivirus protection, and so on designed to secure internet communication.

2. SHTTP includes data entry forms that are used to input data, which has previously been collected into a database. As well as internet-based transactions.
3. SHTTP's services are quite comparable to those of the SSL protocol.
4. Secure HyperText Transfer Protocol works at the application layer (that defines the shared communications protocols and interface methods used by hosts in a network) and is thus closely linked with HTTP.
5. SHTTP can authenticate and encrypt HTTP traffic between the client and the server.
6. SHTTP operates on a message-by-message basis. It can encrypt and sign individual messages.

### Set Protocol

1. Secure Electronic Transaction (SET) is a method that assures the security and integrity of electronic transactions made using credit cards.
2. SET is not a payment system; rather, it is a secure transaction protocol that is used via the internet.
3. The SET protocol provides the following services:

#### *PEM Protocol*

1. PEM Protocol stands for privacy-enhanced mail and is used for email security over the internet.
2. RFC 1421, RFC 1422, RFC 1423, and RFC 1424 are the four particular papers that explain the Privacy Enhanced Mail protocol.
3. It is capable of performing cryptographic operations such as encryption, nonrepudiation, and message integrity.

#### *PGP Protocol*

1. PGP Protocol stands for Pretty Good Privacy, and it is simple to use and free, including its source code documentation.
2. It also meets the fundamental criteria of cryptography.
3. When compared to the PEM protocol, the PGP protocol has grown in popularity and use.
4. The PGP protocol includes cryptographic features such as encryption, non-repudiation, and message integrity.

## 2.4 BIOMETRIC AUTHENTICATION

Biometric authentication is a security process that relies on the unique biological characteristics of individuals to verify they are who they say they are. Biometric authentication systems compare physical or behavioral traits to stored, confirmed, authentic data in a database. If both samples of the biometric data match, authentication is confirmed. Typically, biometric authentication is used to manage access to physical and digital resources, such as buildings, rooms and computing devices. Biometric identification uses biometrics, such as fingerprints, facial recognition or retina scans, to identify a person, whereas biometric authentication is the use of biometrics to verify people are who they claim to be.

## Types of Biometric Authentication

### Chemical Biometric Devices

DNA (deoxyribonucleic acid) matching uses genetic material to identify a person.

### Visual Biometric Devices

1. Retina scans identify subjects by analyzing the unique pattern of blood vessels at the back of their eyes.
2. Iris recognition uses a picture of the iris to identify people in an iris scan.
3. Fingerprint scanners identify people based on their fingerprints.
4. Hand geometry recognition verifies identity or authorizes transactions using a mathematical representation of the unique characteristics of people's hands. This is done by measuring the distances between various parts of the hand, including finger length, finger breadth and the shape of the valleys between the knuckles.
5. Facial recognition relies on the unique characteristics and patterns of people's faces to confirm their identity. The system identifies 80 nodal points on a human face, which make up numeric codes called faceprints.
6. Ear authentication verifies identity based on users' unique ear shape.
7. Signature recognition uses pattern recognition to identify individuals based on their handwritten signature.
8. Vein or vascular scanners
9. Finger vein recognition identifies individuals based on the vein patterns in their finger.

### Behavioral Biometrics

1. Gait analysis examines the way people walk.
2. Typing recognition establishes people's identity based on their unique typing characteristics, including how fast they type.

### Auditory Biometric Devices

Voice ID identifies individuals with voice recognition and relies on characteristics created by the shape of the mouth and throat.

## Biometric Authentication Advantages and Disadvantages

Biometric authentication has its advantages and disadvantages.

The advantages of biometric authentication are its convenience and security. Since biometric authentication uses unique characteristics for verification, they are difficult to replicate. Traditional methods, such as usernames, passwords or ID cards, are not as secure because they can be stolen or guessed easily. In the United States alone, business use of biometric authentication has drastically increased in recent years as more business leaders are becoming more confident in its capabilities.

While biometrics offers many advantages for particular industries, there are controversies surrounding its usage. Organizations may overlook the security of these data-driven security schemes. If bad actors capture biometric data when it is being transmitted to a central database, they can fraudulently replicate that data to perform another transaction. For example, by capturing an individual's fingerprint and using it to access a fingerprint-secured device, hackers or other bad actors could access sensitive data, such as private messages or financial information.

Another potential issue with biometric authentication is that, once a security system has been implemented, an organization may be tempted to use the system for functions beyond its original intention, which is known as function creep. For example, a company may find the technology useful for employee monitoring and management, but once a biometric system has been installed, the organization may find that it has the ability to track exactly where an employee has been.

## 2.5 COMPLIANCE AND SECURITY ASSESSMENT

AI can streamline the compliance process by automating tasks such as data collection, analysis, and reporting. This ensures that organizations meet regulatory requirements more efficiently, reducing the risk of non-compliance penalties and reputational damage.

Business process compliance refers to the process of adhering to rules, policies, standards, and regulations in an organization's day-to-day operations. In most industries, there are rules and guidelines that businesses that operate in the industry must always follow.

As Artificial Intelligence (AI) continues to become more prevalent in the workplace – from recruiting to software development to marketing – organizations are increasingly looking for ways to ensure that their AI systems comply with relevant regulations and standards. The field of AI compliance is complex and ever-changing, and staying up-to-date with the latest developments is essential for any organization that uses artificial intelligence. As a professional – whether you are a manager, developer, security specialist, or simply an AI enthusiast – it is crucial to know what the challenges are in this field and how you can tackle them to save your company money and yourself many headaches.

AI compliance is a process that involves making sure that AI-powered systems are compliant with all applicable laws and regulations.

- It includes checking that companies and individuals do not use AI-powered systems to break any laws or regulations;
- It ensures that the data used to train AI systems is collected and used legally and ethically;
- AI compliance guarantees that AI-powered systems are not used to discriminate against any particular group or individual and are not used to manipulate or deceive people in any way;
- It involves verifying that nobody uses AI-powered systems to invade individuals' privacy or cause any harm to them;
- Finally, AI compliance also assures that AI-powered systems are employed responsibly and in a way that benefits society.

Artificial Intelligence has been at the center of discussions about potential bias in its functioning since the first decade of 2000. There are many examples in which artificial intelligence poses an ethical and security threat, such as:

- AI-based hiring tools. In 2018, Amazon removed a covert AI hiring tool that displayed bias against women. The machine learning model's tendencies caused most ideal candidates to be created as men, reflecting the predominance of men in the computer industry.

- Deepfakes. According to Dr. Tim Stevens (Cyber Security Research Group at King's College London), the use of deepfakes (synthetic media in which the likeness of a different person replaces another in an existing image or video) poses a severe threat to national security since autocracies might make use of them to undermine public confidence in those institutions and organizations.
- AI-powered photo editing and data protection. There have been different examples of dubious handling of data related to apps that use AI to enhance or transform real pictures, such as a Facebook app that leaked data to a Russian company in 2022. Another worrying example was a popular app (FaceApp) which showed a very oddly written privacy policy, stating that any photographs shared by users are effectively the property of FaceApp.

### Role of AI testing in Security Testing

AI can analyze large data sets, such as logs and reports, to identify potential vulnerabilities and threats ahead.

### Use Cases of AI in Security Testing

1. **Hacker behaviour and pattern analysis:** Hackers are always ahead of your team and continuously try to invade. In such cases, it is difficult to understand how a real attacker would behave. With AI in place, you can train AI/ML to identify and exploit vulnerabilities in software systems, which can help security testers understand how an attacker would behave in real-time. This will help you and your team to stay ahead and confront vulnerabilities.
2. **Discovering new vulnerabilities:** Automated security testing has a limitation when it comes to detecting new vulnerabilities. However, AI has the ability to assist in the discovery of previously unknown vulnerabilities. By mimicking human interactions, AI can effectively uncover new vulnerabilities and improve overall efficiency.
3. **Continuously updating test case scenarios based on new vulnerabilities:** AI-powered security testing involves machine learning and threat intelligence. Whenever new security risks arise, AI algorithms examine the most current data to detect patterns and characteristics of these vulnerabilities. AI then produces, examines, and adjusts test cases to address these particular vulnerabilities, ensuring that the testing procedure keeps up with the constantly evolving threat environment.This proactive approach allows organizations to stay ahead of potential security risks and enhance their testing effectiveness.

## 2.6 INTRODUCTION TO PENETRATION TESTING

Penetration testing is a type of security testing that is used to test the insecurity of an application. It is conducted to find the security risk which might be present in the system.

If a system is not secured, then any attacker can disrupt or take authorized access to that system. Security risk is normally an accidental error that occurs while developing and implementing the software. For example, configuration errors, design errors, and software bugs, etc.

Penetration testing normally evaluates a system's ability to protect its networks, applications, endpoints and users from external or internal threats. It also attempts to protect the security controls and ensures only authorized access.

- It identifies a simulation environment i.e., how an intruder may attack the system through white hat attack.
- It helps to find weak areas where an intruder can attack to gain access to the computer's features and data.
- It supports to avoid black hat attack and protects the original data.
- It estimates the magnitude of the attack on potential business.
- It provides evidence to suggest, why it is important to increase investments in security aspect of technology

A white hat hacker -- or ethical hacker -- is an individual who uses hacking skills to identify security vulnerabilities in hardware, software or networks. However, unlike black hat hackers or malicious hackers -white hat hackers respect the rule of law as it applies to hacking. Many white hat hackers are former black hat hackers. The terms come from old Western movies, where heroes often wore white hats and the bad guys wore black hats.

### When to Perform Penetration Testing?

Penetration testing is an essential feature that needs to be performed regularly for securing the functioning of a system. In addition to this, it should be performed whenever –

- Security system discovers new threats by attackers.
- You add a new network infrastructure.
- You update your system or install new software.
- You relocate your office.
- You set up a new end-user program/policy.

**Penetration testing offers the following benefits:**

- **Enhancement of the Management System:** It provides detailed information about the security threats. In addition to this, it also categorizes the degree of vulnerabilities and suggests you, which one is more vulnerable and which one is less. So, you can easily and accurately manage your security system by allocating the security resources accordingly.
- **Avoid Fines:** Penetration testing keeps your organization's major activities updated and complies with the auditing system. So, penetration testing protects you from giving fines.
- **Protection from Financial Damage:** A simple breach of security system may cause millions of dollars of damage. Penetration testing can protect your organization from such damages.
- **Customer Protection:** Breach of even a single customer's data may cause big financial damage as well as reputation damage. It protects the organizations who deal with the customers and keep their data intact.

## 2.7 ACTIVE DIRECTORY SECURITY ASSESSMENT (ADSA)

An Active Directory Security Assessment helps an organization to identify, quantify and reduce the risks affecting the security of one of the most critical infrastructure components in most IT environments. Active Directory (AD) security refers to cybersecurity measures and practices implemented to protect a business network's Microsoft Active Directory infrastructure.

Active Directory was developed by Microsoft to easily manage and organize information about users, computers, and other resources within a network.

AD security plays a central role in authentication, authorization, and the overall security of a Windows-based environment.

Security Active Directory is vital to prevent data breaches and unauthorized access to data, maintain system uptime, and more.

Critical aspects of Active Directory security include:

- **Authentication:** Ensure only authorized users and devices can access your network and resources. This involves using strong passwords, multi-factor authentication (MFA), and other authentication mechanisms.
- **Access Control and Authorization:** Controlling and managing the permissions assigned to users and groups within the Active Directory, ensuring that users have the appropriate level of access to resources. Implementing access controls and least privilege principles to restrict access to sensitive resources and data, reducing the risk of unauthorized access.
- **Group Policies:** Implement and enforce group policies to control and configure user and computer settings. Group Policies help enforce security settings, such as password policies, account lockout policies, and other security configurations.
- **Auditing and Monitoring:** Enabling auditing features to track and monitor activities within the Active Directory environment. This includes logging events related to authentication, changes in permissions, and other security-relevant events.
- **Security Patching and Updates:** Regularly apply security patches and updates to the Active Directory servers and associated systems to address vulnerabilities and ensure a secure operating environment.
- **Secure Communication:** Configuring secure communication channels between Active Directory components to protect against eavesdropping and man-in-the-middle attacks.

This often involves using protocols like Kerberos and implementing encryption mechanisms.

- **Firewall and Network Segmentation:** Employ firewalls and network segmentation to control traffic between different network parts and limit the attack surface.
- **Regular Security Assessments:** Conduct regular security audits and assessments to identify vulnerabilities, misconfigurations, or potential security risks within the Active Directory infrastructure.
- **Backup and Recovery:** Implement robust backup and recovery mechanisms to ensure the availability and integrity of Active Directory data in the event of data loss, corruption, or a security incident.

Active Directory is a widely used directory service crucial in managing and organizing network resources in a Windows environment, including user accounts, computers, and applications.

### Outsource Active Directory Security Management

Yes, it is common for organizations to hire third-party vendors or managed security service providers (MSSPs) to assist with managing Active Directory (AD) security.

These third-party providers often specialize in IT security services and can help ensure the proper configuration, monitoring, and maintenance of Active Directory to enhance security.

Here are some common ways an MSSP (Managed Security Service Provider (MSSP)) can assist you with Active Directory security:

- **Security Assessment and Auditing:** Third-party providers can perform security assessments and audits of your Active Directory environment to identify vulnerabilities, misconfigurations, and areas for improvement.
- **Implementation of Best Practices:** They can help implement best practices for securing Active Directory, including proper user and group management, password policies, and access controls.
- **Monitoring and Incident Response:** Third-party providers may offer continuous monitoring services to detect and respond to security incidents in real-time. This includes monitoring for unusual activities, unauthorized access, and potential security breaches.
- **Patch Management:** Ensuring that Active Directory servers are up-to-date with the latest security patches is crucial. Third-party providers can assist in managing the patching process to minimize vulnerabilities.
- **User Training and Education:** Many security incidents stem from human error. Third- party providers may offer training and educational programs to help users and IT staff understand and adhere to security best practices.
- **Threat Intelligence Integration:** Integrating threat intelligence feeds can enhance the ability to detect and respond to emerging security threats. Third-party providers can help implement and manage these integrations.

When considering hiring a third party for Active Directory security management, choosing a reputable and experienced provider is important. Ensure they have a good track record in the industry, understand your organization's specific needs, and comply with any regulatory requirements that may apply to your industry.

Before entering into any agreement, it's also advisable to define clear service level agreements (SLAs) and establish communication channels to ensure a smooth collaboration between your organization and the third-party provider.

## 2.8 CYBER INSURANCE RISK ASSESSMENT

Practically every organization has internet connectivity and some form of IT infrastructure, which means nearly all organizations are at risk of a cyberattack. To understand how great this risk is and to be able to manage it, organizations need to complete a cybersecurity risk assessment, a process that identifies which assets are most vulnerable to the cyber-risks the organization faces.

This is a risk assessment that looks specifically at cyber threats, so risks such as fire and flooding -- which would be included in a general risk assessment -- are not in scope.

Mitigating the risks identified during the assessment will prevent and reduce costly security incidents and data breaches, and avoid regulatory and compliance issues. The risk assessment process also obliges everyone within an organization to consider how cybersecurity risks can impact the organization's objectives, which helps to create a more risk-aware culture. So, what is at the heart of a cybersecurity risk assessment?

A cybersecurity risk assessment can be split into many parts, but the five main steps are:

## Scoping, Risk identification, Risk analysis, Risk evaluation and Documentation

### Step 1: Determine the Scope of the Risk Assessment

A risk assessment starts by deciding what is in scope of the assessment. It could be the entire organization, but this is usually too big an undertaking, so it is more likely to be a business unit, location or a specific aspect of the business, such as payment processing or a web application.

It is vital to have the full support of all stakeholders whose activities are within the scope of the assessment, as their input will be essential to understanding which assets and processes are the most important, identifying risks, assessing impacts and defining risk tolerance levels. A third party specializing in risk assessments might be needed to help them through what is a resource-intensive exercise.

Everyone involved should be familiar with the terminology used in a risk assessment, such as likelihood and impact, so that there is a common understanding of how the risk is framed. For those who are unfamiliar with cybersecurity concepts, ISO/IEC TS 27100 provides a useful overview. Prior to undertaking a risk assessment, it is well worth reviewing standards like ISO/IEC 27001 and frameworks such as NIST SP 800-37 and ISO/IEC TS 27110, which can help guide organizations on how to assess their information security risks in a structured manner and ensure mitigating controls are appropriate and effective.

Various standards and laws such as HIPAA, Sarbanes-Oxley and PCI DSS require organizations to complete a formalized risk assessment and often provide guidelines and recommendations on how to complete them. However, avoid a compliance-oriented, checklist approach when undertaking an assessment, as simply fulfilling compliance requirements doesn't necessarily mean an organization is not exposed to any risks.

### Step 2: How to Identify Cybersecurity Risks

You can't protect what you don't know, so the next task is to identify and create an inventory of all physical and logical assets that are within the scope of the risk assessment. When identifying assets, it is important to not only establish those that are considered the organization's crown jewels -- assets critical to the business and probably the main target of attackers -- but also assets attackers would want to take control over, such as an Active Directory server or picture archive and communications systems, to use as a pivot point to expand an attack. Creating a network architecture diagram from the asset inventory list is a great way to visualize the interconnectivity and communication paths between assets and processes as well as entry points into the network, making the next task of identifying threats easier.

## Identify Threats

Threats are the tactics, techniques and methods used by threat actors that have the potential to cause harm to an organization's assets. To help identify potential threats to each asset, use a threat library such as the Mitre ATT&CK Knowledge Base and resources from the Cyber Threat Alliance, which both provide high-quality, up-to-date cyberthreat information. Security vendor reports and advisories from government agencies such as the Cybersecurity & Infrastructure Security Agency can be an excellent source of news on new threats surfacing in specific industries, verticals and geographic regions or particular technologies.

Also consider where each asset sits in the Lockheed Martin cyber kill chain, as this will help determine the types of protection they need. The cyber kill chain maps out the stages and objectives of a typical real-world attack.

Developed by Lockheed Martin, the Cyber Kill Chain® framework is part of the Intelligence Driven Defense® model for identification and prevention of cyber intrusions activity. The model identifies what the adversaries must complete in order to achieve their objective.

This task involves specifying the consequences of an identified threat exploiting a vulnerability to attack an in-scope asset. For example, consider the following scenario:

- **Threat:** An attacker performs a SQL injection.
- **Vulnerability/asset:** Unpatched web server.
- **Consequence:** Customers' private data stolen, resulting in regulatory fines and damage to reputation.

Now it is time to determine the likelihood of the risk scenarios documented in Step 2 actually occurring, and the impact on the organization if it did happen. In a cybersecurity risk assessment, risk likelihood -- the probability that a given threat is capable of exploiting a given vulnerability -- should be determined based on the discoverability, exploitability and reproducibility of threats and vulnerabilities rather than historical occurrences. This is because the dynamic nature of cybersecurity threats means likelihood is not so closely linked to the frequency of past occurrences in the way that flooding and earthquakes.

Impact refers to the magnitude of harm to the organization resulting from the consequences of a threat exploiting a vulnerability. The impact on confidentiality, integrity and availability should be assessed in each scenario with the highest impact used as the final score.

This aspect of the assessment is subjective in nature, which is why input from stakeholders and security experts is so important. Taking the SQL injection above, the impact rating on confidentiality would probably be ranked as "Very Severe."

## Determine and Prioritize Risks

Using a risk matrix like the one below where the risk level is "Likelihood times Impact," each risk scenario can be classified. If the risk of a SQL injection attack were considered "Likely" or "Highly Likely" our example risk scenario would be classified as "Very High."

Any scenario that is above the agreed-upon tolerance level should be prioritized for treatment to bring it within the organization's risk tolerance level. The following are three ways of doing this:

1. **Avoid.** If the risk outweighs the benefits, discontinuing an activity may be the best course of action if it means no longer being exposed to it.
2. **Transfer.** Share a portion of the risk with other parties through outsourcing certain operations to third parties, such as DDoS mitigation or purchasing cyber insurance. First- party coverage generally only covers the costs incurred due to a cyber event, such as informing customers about a data breach, while third-party coverage would cover the cost of funding a settlement after a data breach along with penalties and fines. What it will not cover are the intangible costs of loss of intellectual property or damage to brand reputation.
3. **Mitigate.** Deploy security controls and other measures to reduce the likelihood and/or effect and therefore the risk level to within the agreed risk tolerance level. Responsibility for implementing the measures to reduce unacceptably high risks should be assigned to the appropriate team. Dates for progress and completion reports should also be set to ensure that the owner of the risk and the treatment plan are kept up to date.

However, no system or environment can be made 100% secure, so there is always some risk left over. This is called residual risk and must be formally accepted by senior stakeholders as part of the organization's cybersecurity strategy.

## Document All Risks

It's important to document all identified risk scenarios in a risk register. This should be regularly reviewed and updated to ensure that management always has an up-to-date account of its cybersecurity risks. It should include the following:

- Risk scenario.
- Identification date.
- Existing security controls.
- Current risk level.
- Treatment plan, meaning the planned activities and timeline to bring the risk within an acceptable risk tolerance level along with the commercial justification for the investment.
- Progress status, as in the status of implementing the treatment plan.
- Residual risk, or the risk level after the treatment plan is implemented.
- Risk owner, meaning the individual or group responsible for ensuring that the residual risks remain within the tolerance level.

A cybersecurity risk assessment is a large and ongoing undertaking, so time and resources need to be made available if it is going to improve the future security of the organization. It will need to be repeated as new cyber threats arise and new systems or activities are introduced; but, done well the first time around, it will provide a repeatable process and template for future assessments, while reducing the chances of a cyberattack adversely affecting business objectives.

◆◆◆

*Intentionally left blank!*

3

UNIT

# Impact of AI on Cybersecurity

## 3.1 THREAT HUNTING IN MEMORY

### Threat Hunting Definition

This can be done by: Checking your system's memory for malicious activity using memory dumps, which are snapshots of a device's random access memory (RAM) at a specific point in time. Analyzing server images for threat activity. Checking endpoint protection data for signs of suspicious. Threat hunting in memory is a crucial aspect of cybersecurity, especially when dealing with AI-enhanced cyber threats. Memory-based attacks, also known as file less attacks, exploit vulnerabilities in a system's memory rather than relying on traditional methods like malicious files. AI-enhanced cyber threats can make these attacks more sophisticated and harder to detect. Here are some strategies for threat hunting in memory, particularly in the context of AI- enhanced threats:

### Behavioral Analysis

Leverage AI and machine learning algorithms to establish a baseline of normal behavior for processes and applications in the system's memory. **Monitor for any deviations** from the established baseline, as anomalies may indicate malicious activity.

### Endpoint Detection and Response (EDR) Solutions

Deploy EDR solutions that specifically focus on monitoring and responding to activities in memory. These solutions often use advanced heuristics and behavior analysis, including AI algorithms, to detect and respond to suspicious activities.

### Memory Forensics

- FTK Imager, Volatility, Memory acquisition --- tools.
- Utilize memory forensics tools to analyze the content of a system's memory in real-time.
- Look for signs of in-memory attacks, such as injected code, unusual API calls, or unauthorized changes to memory regions.
- API stands for Application Programming Interface.

### Sandboxes and Emulation

Use sandbox environments or emulation tools to execute and analyze potentially malicious code in a controlled setting.

This helps identify memory-based attacks that might otherwise go undetected in traditional environments.

### Pattern Recognition

Train AI models to recognize patterns associated with memory-based attacks.

Regularly update these models to adapt to evolving attack techniques and improve the accuracy of threat detection.

### Network Traffic Analysis

Monitor network traffic for unusual patterns or behaviors that may indicate memory-based attacks.

Integrating AI algorithms can enhance the ability to identify patterns that may be indicative of advanced threats.

### Threat Intelligence Integration

Integrate threat intelligence feeds with AI capabilities to enhance the detection of known memory-based attack patterns.

Stay updated on the latest threat intelligence to proactively defend against emerging threats.

### User and Entity Behavior Analytics (UEBA)

Employ UEBA solutions that use AI to analyze the behavior of users and entities within the organization.

Identify deviations from normal behavior, which could be indicative of a memory-based attack.

### Continuous Monitoring and Response

Implement continuous monitoring of memory activities and establish a rapid response mechanism to contain and mitigate any identified threats.

### Education and Training

Ensure that security teams are well-trained in identifying and responding to memory-based attacks, including those enhanced by AI.

By combining these strategies, organizations can strengthen their ability to detect and respond to memory-based attacks, even when amplified by AI-enhanced cyber threats. Regularly updating defenses and staying informed about emerging threats are essential components of an effective cybersecurity strategy.

## 3.2 FILE SYSTEM AND NETWORK DATA

### 3.2.1 File System

AI-enhanced cyber threats often leverage both file system and network data to carry out attacks. Understanding and monitoring these aspects are crucial for effective cybersecurity. Here are some considerations for dealing with file system and network data in the context of AI-enhanced threats:

### File System Data

Employ AI algorithms to analyze the behavior of files and processes on the file system. Identify patterns associated with malicious activities, such as unauthorized access, file modifications, or the creation of suspicious files.

### Endpoint Protection

Utilize AI-driven endpoint protection solutions that can detect and block malicious files based on their behavior.Implement real-time scanning and analysis of files to identify and mitigate threats before they can execute.

### File Integrity Monitoring (FIM)

Implement FIM solutions to monitor changes to critical files and directories. Leverage AI to detect anomalies in file changes that may indicate a compromise.

### Malware Detection and Analysis

Use AI-enhanced malware detection tools to identify and analyze malicious files.These tools can leverage machine learning to recognize new and evolving patterns of malware.

### Sandboxing

Employ sandboxing techniques to execute and analyze suspicious files in a controlled environment. AI can enhance the analysis of file behavior within the sandbox, helping to identify sophisticated threats.

### Threat Intelligence Integration

Integrate threat intelligence feeds with AI capabilities to identify files associated with known threats. Regularly update threat intelligence databases to stay informed about the latest indicators of compromise.

## 3.2.2 Network Data

Use AI-driven network traffic analysis to detect anomalies in communication patterns. Identify unusual data flows, connections to malicious domains, or patterns indicative of lateral movement.

### Intrusion Detection Systems (IDS)

Implement IDS solutions that leverage AI to detect and respond to suspicious network activities.Train AI models on historical data to improve the accuracy of identifying abnormal network behavior.

### User and Entity Behavior Analytics (UEBA)

Integrate UEBA solutions with network data to analyze the behavior of users and entities. Identify deviations from normal behavior that may indicate a compromised system or user account.

### Deep Packet Inspection

Utilize deep packet inspection with AI for more granular analysis of network traffic.Identify patterns associated with advanced threats, such as command and control communication or data exfiltration.

### *Network Segmentation*

Implement network segmentation to limit the lateral movement of threats within the network. AI can assist in dynamically adjusting segmentation based on real-time threat assessments.

### *Cloud Security Monitoring*

Extend network monitoring capabilities to include cloud environments. Leverage AI to detect and respond to threats in cloud-based infrastructure and services.

### *Incident Response Automation*

Integrate AI into incident response workflows to automate the identification and containment of network-based threats.

### *Continuous Monitoring*

Establish continuous monitoring practices for network data to ensure timely detection of potential threats.

By combining AI-driven analysis of both file system and network data, organizations can enhance their ability to detect and respond to AI-enhanced cyber threats. Regularly updating and fine-tuning AI models based on evolving threats is crucial for maintaining the effectiveness of these cybersecurity measures.

## 3.3 INTRODUCTORY ANALYSIS OF MALICIOUS PROGRAMS

Malicious programs, commonly known as malware, are software applications designed to infiltrate, damage, or disrupt computer systems, networks, and devices. Cybercriminals use these programs to steal sensitive data, cause financial losses, or take control of targeted systems for malicious purposes. The landscape of malware has evolved significantly, from early computer viruses and worms to sophisticated, AI-powered cyber threats that can adapt to security defenses in real time.

Malware can be categorized into various types, including **viruses**, which attach themselves to legitimate files and spread upon execution; **worms,** which self-replicate and spread across networks without user intervention; **Trojans**, which disguise themselves as legitimate software to deceive users; **ransomware**, which encrypts files and demands payment for decryption; and **rootkits,** which provide unauthorized access to attackers while remaining hidden from detection tools. Additionally, modern threats such as **file less malware**, which operates directly in system memory without leaving a traceable file, and **polymorphic malware,** which constantly changes its code to evade detection, pose significant challenges for traditional security solutions.

Malware can be categorized into several types based on its behavior and attack methodology:

1. **Viruses:** Self-replicating programs that attach themselves to legitimate files and spread when executed.
2. **Worms:** Standalone programs that propagate across networks without user intervention.
3. **Trojans:** Malicious programs disguised as legitimate software, often used for backdoor access.

4. **Ransomware** – Encrypts a victim's files and demands payment for decryption, causing financial and operational damage.
5. **Spyware:** Secretly monitors user activity, collecting sensitive information such as passwords and financial data.
6. **Rootkits:** Hide deep within operating systems to provide persistent access to attackers while avoiding detection.
7. **Adware:** Displays unwanted advertisements and may track user behavior for targeted marketing or further exploitation.
8. **File less Malware:** Operates directly in system memory, making it difficult for traditional antivirus solutions to detect.
9. **Polymorphic and Metamorphic Malware:** Modifies its code to evade signature-based detection mechanisms.

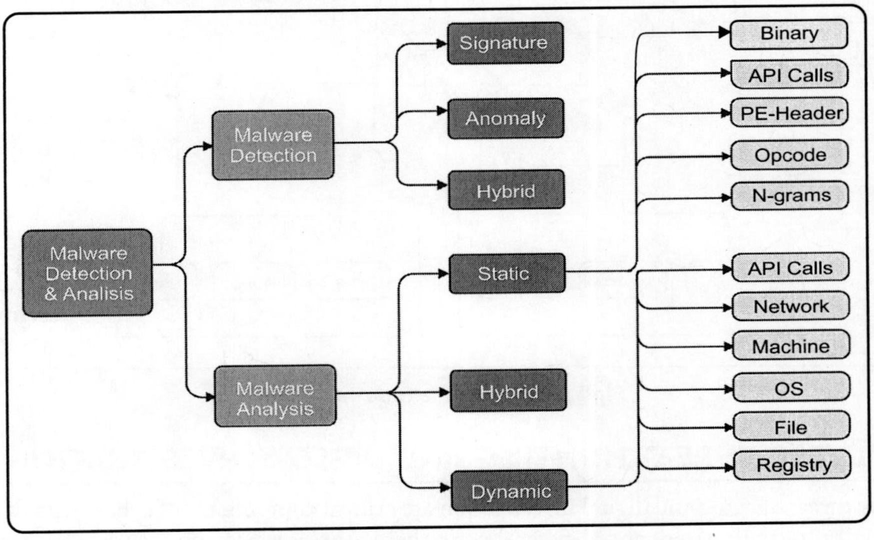


***Fig 3.1** Malware Detection and Analysis*

With the rise of AI in cybersecurity, threat actors are leveraging machine learning and deep learning techniques to create more advanced malware that can bypass traditional security measures. AI-powered malware can modify its behavior based on the environment it operates in, making it difficult to detect using signature-based antivirus solutions. Similarly, adversarial AI techniques allow malware to evade detection by manipulating AI-based security systems and learning how they operate.

To counter these threats, security researchers and organizations are adopting AI-driven threat intelligence, anomaly detection, and behavioral analysis to identify and mitigate malware attacks effectively. Advanced cybersecurity techniques such as heuristic analysis, sandboxing, and machine learning models are now essential in detecting and neutralizing malicious programs before they can cause significant harm. As cyber threats continue to evolve, understanding the fundamentals of malware, its attack mechanisms, and AI-driven defense strategies remains crucial in building a secure digital ecosystem.

To combat these evolving threats, security professionals employ behavioral analysis, heuristic detection, sandboxing, and AI-driven cybersecurity tools. AI is now being integrated into threat intelligence systems to predict, detect, and mitigate malware attacks in real time. As cybercriminals continue to leverage AI to develop more advanced threats, a proactive and adaptive security approach is necessary to safeguard digital ecosystems against malicious programs.

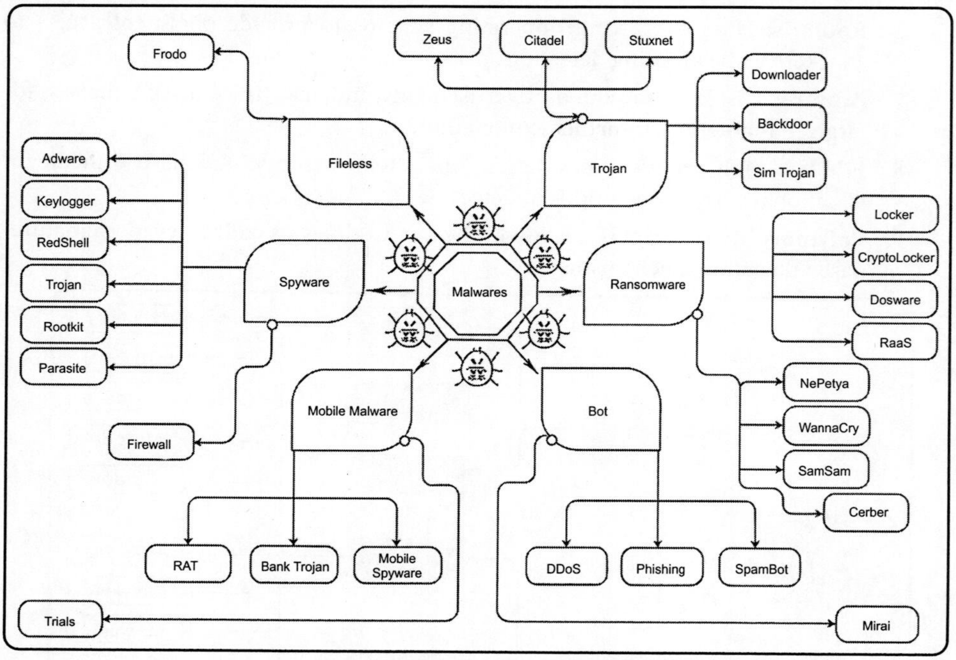


***Fig : 3.2** Modern Malware Taxanomy*

## 3.4 CYBER THREAT HUNTING AND DIGITAL INVESTIGATION

Cyber threat hunting and digital investigation are critical components of cybersecurity, and when dealing with AI-enhanced cyber threats, these processes become even more complex. Threat hunting involves actively searching for signs of malicious activity within a network, while digital investigation focuses on analyzing and responding to security incidents. Incorporating AI into these practices can enhance the efficiency and effectiveness of cyber threat hunting and digital investigation.

### Cyber Threat Hunting

#### *AI-Driven Analytics*

Utilize AI algorithms for advanced analytics to identify patterns, anomalies, and potential threats within large datasets. Train AI models to recognize known threat indicators and behaviors associated with AI- enhanced cyber threats.

#### *Automated Threat Detection*

Implement automated threat detection mechanisms powered by AI to continuously monitor network traffic, logs, and other data sources. Leverage machine learning models to autonomously identify suspicious activities and potential threats.

### Behavioral Analysis

Employ AI for behavioral analysis to establish baselines for normal network and user behavior. Identify deviations from these baselines as potential indicators of compromise during threat hunting activities.

### Threat Intelligence Integration

Integrate AI-enhanced threat intelligence feeds to stay updated on the latest information about emerging threats.Automatically correlate threat intelligence with observed activities during threat hunting operations.

### Data Correlation and Enrichment

Use AI to correlate data from various sources and enrich the context of security events. Enhance the speed and accuracy of identifying relationships between seemingly disparate events.

### Predictive Analysis

Leverage AI for predictive analysis to identify potential future threats based on historical data and emerging trends. Anticipate and proactively address potential vulnerabilities or attack vectors.

### Automated Response

Integrate AI-driven automated response mechanisms to quickly contain and remediate identified threats. Enable real-time decision-making for incident response based on AI analysis.

### Digital Investigation: Forensic Analysis with AI

Incorporate AI into forensic analysis tools to speed up the examination of digital evidence. Use AI for file analysis, memory forensics, and identification of artifacts associated with AI- enhanced attacks.

### Pattern Recognition

Train AI models to recognize patterns of attack in digital forensics data, such as malware signatures or attacker. Accelerate the identification of malicious activities through automated pattern recognition.

### Timeline Analysis

Employ AI to analyze timelines of events during a security incident, helping investigators reconstruct the sequence of actions taken by attackers. Identify the root cause and the extent of the impact of an AI-enhanced cyber threat.

### Data Correlation

Utilize AI for correlating digital evidence across different sources, including network logs, endpoint data, and cloud services. Identify the full scope of the incident by connecting relevant pieces of information.

### *Natural Language Processing (NLP)*

Implement NLP capabilities to analyze and understand text-based evidence, such as chat logs or communication records.Extract meaningful insights and context from unstructured data during digital investigations.

### *Automated Reporting*

Integrate AI into reporting processes to automate the generation of detailed and structured reports. Facilitate communication with stakeholders and regulatory bodies with clear and timely information.

### *Continuous Improvement*

Continuously train and update AI models based on the evolving nature of AI-enhanced cyber threats. Use feedback from digital investigations to enhance the accuracy of AI algorithms and improve detection capabilities. By combining AI with cyber threat hunting and digital investigation practices, organizations can enhance their ability to detect, respond to, and recover from AI-enhanced cyber threats. Regular training, adaptation, and collaboration between human analysts and AI systems are essential for maintaining an effective cybersecurity posture.

## 3.5 DETAILED ANALYSIS OF REAL-WORLD CASE STUDIES

The increasing integration of Artificial Intelligence (AI) in cybersecurity has led to both advancements in defense mechanisms and new, sophisticated cyber threats. Real-world case studies highlight how AI-powered attacks and defenses shape the evolving cybersecurity landscape. Below are some notable examples of AI-driven cyber threats and their countermeasures.

### DeepLocker (2018) – AI-Powered Malware

DeepLocker, an AI-driven polymorphic malware developed as a proof-of-concept by IBM researchers, demonstrated how AI can be used to evade traditional security solutions. This malware used deep learning-based trigger conditions, such as facial recognition, geolocation, or specific behavior patterns, to remain dormant until it reached its target.

- Unlike traditional malware, DeepLocker avoided detection by remaining inactive until precise conditions were met.
- The attack vector demonstrated how AI could be weaponized for targeted cyber espionage and undetectable payload delivery.
- AI-based behavioral anomaly detection to track unusual system behavior.
- Zero-trust security frameworks to limit malware execution permissions.

### TrickBot and AI-Driven Phishing Attacks

TrickBot is a modular banking Trojan that has evolved to use machine learning (ML) techniques for phishing campaigns. By analyzing user behavior, email patterns, and language nuances, TrickBot-generated phishing emails became more convincing and harder to detect.

- Victims unknowingly provided credentials, leading to financial fraud and corporate espionage.
- TrickBot infected millions of devices worldwide, contributing to the spread of ransomware like Ryuk.
- AI-driven email filtering and anomaly detection to flag suspicious messages.
- User behavior analytics (UBA) to detect unauthorized account access.

## Emotet – AI-Powered Malware-as-a-Service (MaaS)

Emotet evolved into a self-propagating AI-enhanced botnet, distributing malware through malicious email attachments. It used AI-driven social engineering tactics to create highly personalized phishing messages.

- Spread across government agencies and financial institutions, leading to significant data breaches.
- Used machine learning-based evasion techniques to bypass traditional antivirus solutions.
- AI-powered threat intelligence platforms to identify and block Emotet's evolving attack strategies.
- Automated malware analysis and sandboxing to prevent execution of malicious payloads.

## AI in Defending Against Advanced Persistent Threats (APTs) – The Solar Winds Attack (2020)

The SolarWinds supply chain attack was a highly sophisticated APT where attackers infiltrated government agencies and private corporations by injecting malware into legitimate software updates.

- The attack went undetected for several months, affecting thousands of organizations worldwide.
- Traditional security tools failed to recognize the slow and stealthy nature of the attack.
- Machine learning anomaly detection helped security teams identify unusual network activity.
- AI-enhanced Security Information and Event Management (SIEM) systems flagged irregular access patterns.

## AI in IoT Security – The Mirai Botnet Attack (2016)

Mirai exploited IoT devices with default credentials, creating a botnet that launched massive Distributed Denial-of-Service (DDoS) attacks. AI-powered malware variations later made Mirai more evasive and adaptive.

- Caused the largest DDoS attack in history, taking down major services like Dyn, Netflix, and Twitter.
- Highlighted vulnerabilities in IoT security due to weak authentication and default passwords.

## 3.6 UNUSUAL AND NON-VIRULENT TYPES OF MALWARE: KNN (K - NEAREST NEIGHBOURS) FOR THREAT VISUALIZERS

K-Nearest Neighbors (KNN) is a machine learning algorithm commonly used for classification and regression tasks. While it's not typically associated with malware detection or threat visualization, it's an interesting concept to explore how machine learning techniques can be applied in the context of cybersecurity. Here's a hypothetical scenario of how KNN could be utilized in threat visualization:

- **Feature Extraction:** Extract relevant features from malware samples or system data. These features could include various characteristics such as file size, API calls, system calls, network activity, etc.
- **Feature Vector Creation:** Represent each malware sample or system data point as a feature vector, where each feature corresponds to one of the extracted characteristics.
- **Training Phase:** Train the KNN model using a labeled dataset of known malware samples and benign software. The model learns to classify new samples based on their similarity to the training data.
- **Visualization:** Once the KNN model is trained, visualize the decision boundaries it creates in the feature space. This can provide insights into how the model distinguishes between different classes (malware vs. benign).
- **Real-time Monitoring:** Deploy the trained model in a real-time monitoring system where it can classify incoming samples or system data and visualize potential threats based on their proximity to known malware samples in the feature space.

It's important to note that while KNN can be effective for certain types of classification tasks, it may not be the most suitable approach for detecting sophisticated or polymorphic malware variants. Additionally, the effectiveness of any machine learning-based approach relies heavily on the quality of the features used and the representativeness of the training data.

In summary, while KNN for threat visualization presents an interesting concept, it's essential to complement it with other techniques and methodologies to build robust and effective cybersecurity systems. Malware, short for malicious software, refers to any type of software intentionally designed to cause harm to a computer, server, network, or user. Malware encompasses a wide range of malicious programs, each with its own specific functionalities and objectives.

Some common types of malware include:

- **Viruses:** A virus is a program that can replicate itself and spread to other files or computers. Viruses often attach themselves to executable files and can cause damage by corrupting or deleting data, or by interfering with system operations.
- **Worms:** Worms are standalone programs that replicate themselves over a network, spreading from one system to another without requiring human interaction. Worms can consume network bandwidth and degrade system performance, and they may also carry payloads that perform other malicious activities.
- **Trojans:** Trojans are programs that appear to be legitimate but contain malicious code. Unlike viruses and worms, Trojans do not replicate themselves. Instead,

they typically trick users into executing them by disguising themselves as useful software or by exploiting vulnerabilities in legitimate programs.

- **Ransomware:** Ransomware is a type of malware that encrypts the victim's files or locks their system, rendering it unusable. The attacker then demands a ransom payment in exchange for restoring access to the affected files or system. Ransomware attacks can have devastating consequences for individuals and organizations alike.
- **Spyware:** Spyware is software that secretly monitors a user's activities and collects sensitive information such as login credentials, financial data, or browsing history. This information is then sent to a remote server controlled by the attacker. Spyware can compromise user privacy and security.
- **Adware:** Adware is software that displays unwanted advertisements to the user, often in the form of pop-up windows or browser redirects. While not necessarily harmful in itself, adware can be intrusive and disruptive, and it may also collect user data without consent.

These are just a few examples of the many types of malware that exist. Malware authors continually evolve their techniques and develop new variants to evade detection and maximize their impact. As such, combating malware requires a multi-layered approach that includes robust cybersecurity measures, user education, and proactive threat detection and response strategies.

## Exploring How KNN Could Be Used In Threat Visualization

In the realm of AI-enhanced cyber threats, there's an evolving landscape of unconventional and non-virulent malware types that leverage sophisticated techniques to evade detection and exploit vulnerabilities. Let's explore how K-Nearest Neighbors (KNN) could potentially be used in threat visualization within this context:

- **Polymorphic Malware:** Polymorphic malware constantly changes its appearance to evade signature-based detection methods. Instead of exhibiting a fixed set of characteristics, polymorphic malware alters its code or behavior with each infection. KNN could be employed to analyze patterns in the behavior or structure of polymorphic malware and visualize the variations over time, helping cybersecurity analysts identify commonalities or trends that indicate malicious activity.
- **Fileless Malware:** Fileless malware operates entirely in memory, leaving little to no footprint on disk, making it difficult to detect using traditional antivirus solutions. KNN could analyze system activity and behavior, such as process memory usage, API calls, and network traffic patterns, to identify anomalies indicative of fileless malware attacks. Visualizing these anomalies in real-time can assist analysts in identifying and responding to emerging threats promptly.
- **AI-Generated Malware:** With advancements in artificial intelligence, there's a growing concern about AI-generated malware designed to exploit vulnerabilities or bypass security defenses. KNN could be utilized to analyze the characteristics of AI-generated malware samples and create a visual representation of their features and similarities. This visualization can aid researchers in understanding the underlying patterns and behaviors of AI-generated threats, enabling the development of more effective detection and mitigation strategies.

- **IoT Botnets:** Internet of Things (IoT) botnets leverage compromised IoT devices to launch large-scale distributed denial-of-service (DDoS) attacks or propagate malware. KNN could be applied to analyze network traffic data from IoT devices and visualize the communication patterns between compromised devices and command-and-control servers. By identifying clusters of suspicious activity in the visualization, security teams can proactively mitigate IoT botnet attacks and secure vulnerable devices.
- **AI-Driven Social Engineering Attacks:** AI-enhanced social engineering attacks utilize machine learning algorithms to craft convincing phishing emails or messages tailored to specific individuals or organizations. KNN could analyze the linguistic characteristics and content of phishing attempts to detect subtle deviations from legitimate communication patterns. Visualizing these deviations can help users and security professionals identify suspicious messages and mitigate the risk of falling victim to social engineering attacks.

Incorporating KNN-based threat visualization into AI-enhanced cybersecurity solutions can provide valuable insights into emerging threats and enable proactive threat detection and response. However, it's essential to continuously adapt and refine these techniques to keep pace with the evolving landscape of cyber threats. Collaboration between cybersecurity experts, data scientists, and AI researchers is crucial to effectively combatting sophisticated and unconventional malware threats.

## 3.7 ISOLATION FOREST FOR ANOMALY DETECTION

Isolation in the context of AI-enhanced cyber threats typically refers to the practice of containing or segregating potentially malicious activities, files, or processes to prevent them from causing harm to the rest of the system or network. This isolation can take various forms and may involve both manual intervention by cybersecurity professionals and automated responses implemented by security systems. Here's how isolation can be applied in the context of AI-enhanced cyber threats:

- **Sandboxing:** Sandboxing involves running potentially malicious files or processes in a controlled environment, known as a sandbox, where their behavior can be monitored and analyzed without posing a risk to the underlying system. AI algorithms can be used to automatically analyze the behavior of suspicious files or processes within the sandbox, identifying indicators of compromise or malicious activity. If deemed safe, the file or process may be allowed to execute outside the sandbox; otherwise, it may be isolated to prevent further harm.
- **Microsegmentation:** Microsegmentation involves dividing a network into smaller, isolated segments to contain the spread of cyber threats. AI algorithms can be employed to continuously monitor network traffic and detect anomalous behavior indicative of a cyber attack. If a threat is identified within a particular network segment, AI-driven security systems can automatically isolate that segment from the rest of the network to prevent lateral movement and limit the impact of the attack.
- **Virtualization:** Virtualization technologies allow the creation of isolated virtual environments within a single physical server or workstation. AI-enhanced security solutions can leverage virtualization to isolate potentially compromised systems or processes, preventing them from accessing critical resources or sensitive data.

Virtualized environments can be automatically spun up or torn down based on AI-driven threat intelligence, enabling rapid response to emerging cyber threats.

- **Containerization:** Containerization platforms such as Docker provide lightweight, isolated environments for running applications and services. AI algorithms can be integrated into container orchestration systems to continuously monitor the behavior of containerized applications and detect signs of malicious activity. If a container is identified as compromised, AI-driven security mechanisms can isolate it from other containers and the host system to mitigate the risk of further exploitation.
- **Endpoint Isolation:** Endpoint isolation involves quarantining potentially compromised devices, such as desktops, laptops, or mobile devices, to prevent them from accessing the corporate network or spreading malware to other endpoints. AI-powered endpoint detection and response (EDR) solutions can automatically identify suspicious behavior on endpoints and trigger isolation measures to contain the threat while investigation and remediation take place.

In summary, isolation plays a critical role in mitigating AI-enhanced cyber threats by containing malicious activities and preventing them from spreading across systems or networks. By integrating AI algorithms into isolation mechanisms, organizations can enhance their ability to detect and respond to cyber threats in real-time, minimizing the impact of security incidents and safeguarding sensitive data and assets.

## 3.7.1 FOREST FOR ANOMALY DETECTION

The "Forest for Anomaly Detection" refers to using ensemble learning techniques like Random Forests for detecting anomalies or unusual behavior in AI-enhanced cybersecurity. Ensemble methods combine multiple models to improve the overall performance and robustness of the anomaly detection system. Here's how a Random Forest approach might be applied in the context of AI-enhanced cyber threats:

- **Feature Extraction:** Relevant features are extracted from various data sources, such as network traffic logs, system event logs, or application behavior. These features could include metrics like packet size, frequency of system calls, login patterns, or resource usage.
- **Training Phase:** A Random Forest model is trained using labeled data, where normal behavior is labeled as "normal" and any deviations from normal behavior are labeled as "anomalous." The model learns to distinguish between normal and anomalous patterns based on the input features.
- **Ensemble Learning:** Random Forest is an ensemble learning technique that combines multiple decision trees to make predictions. Each decision tree is trained on a random subset of the training data and selects a random subset of features at each node. By aggregating the predictions of multiple trees, Random Forest reduces overfitting and improves generalization performance.
- **Anomaly Detection:** During the detection phase, the trained Random Forest model is applied to incoming data in real-time. If the model predicts that a particular data instance deviates significantly from the learned patterns of normal behavior, it is flagged as anomalous and triggers an alert or response mechanism.
- **Continuous Learning:** An AI-enhanced system can continuously adapt and improve its anomaly detection capabilities over time. As new data becomes

available, the Random Forest model can be updated and retrained to incorporate the latest information and adapt to evolving cyber threats.

- **Visualizing Anomalies:** Anomalies detected by the Random Forest model can be visualized to provide cybersecurity analysts with insights into emerging threats and unusual patterns in the data. Visualization techniques such as scatter plots, heatmaps, or time series plots can help analysts understand the nature of the anomalies and prioritize response actions accordingly.

By leveraging ensemble learning techniques like Random Forests for anomaly detection, AI-enhanced cybersecurity systems can effectively identify and mitigate a wide range of cyber threats, including zero-day attacks, insider threats, and sophisticated malware variants. Additionally, the continuous learning capabilities of these systems enable them to adapt to evolving threats and maintain high detection accuracy over time.

## 3.8 LSTM FOR MULTI-VECTOR CORRELATION

Long Short-Term Memory (LSTM) networks are a type of recurrent neural network (RNN) architecture that is particularly effective at capturing sequential patterns and long-range dependencies in time-series data. In the context of AI-enhanced cybersecurity, LSTM networks can be applied for multi-vector correlation, which involves analyzing multiple streams of data to identify correlated patterns indicative of cyber threats. Here's how LSTM can be used for multi-vector correlation in AI-enhanced cyber threat detection:

- **Data Collection:** Various data sources related to cybersecurity, such as network traffic logs, system event logs, intrusion detection system (IDS) alerts, and endpoint telemetry, are collected and preprocessed. Each data source provides a different perspective on the security posture of the system or network.
- **Feature Extraction:** Relevant features are extracted from each data source to create feature vectors. These features could include network traffic attributes (e.g., source IP address, destination port), system call sequences, user authentication logs, and file access patterns.
- **Sequence Modeling with LSTM:** LSTM networks are employed to model the sequential nature of the data from each source. Each LSTM model is trained on sequences of features extracted from a particular data source, enabling it to capture temporal dependencies and patterns within that data stream.
- **Multi-Vector Correlation:** The outputs of the individual LSTM models are then combined and fed into a higher-level LSTM or another neural network architecture for multi-vector correlation. This model learns to identify correlations and relationships between the different data streams, allowing it to detect complex attack patterns that span multiple vectors.
- **Anomaly Detection and Threat Identification:** The multi-vector correlation model is used to analyze incoming data in real-time. If the model detects anomalies or suspicious patterns that exhibit correlated behavior across multiple vectors, it raises an alert or triggers an automated response to mitigate the threat.
- **Feedback Loop and Continuous Learning:** As new data becomes available, the LSTM models are updated and retrained to adapt to evolving cyber threats. This continuous learning process ensures that the multi-vector correlation model remains effective in detecting emerging threats and evolving attack techniques.

- **Visualization and Interpretation:** The correlated patterns identified by the multi-vector correlation model can be visualized to provide cybersecurity analysts with insights into the nature of the threats and the relationships between different data sources. Visualization techniques such as heatmaps, network graphs, or timeline visualizations can help analysts understand the attack lifecycle and prioritize response actions accordingly.

By leveraging LSTM networks for multi-vector correlation, AI-enhanced cybersecurity systems can effectively identify sophisticated cyber threats that involve coordinated attacks across multiple attack vectors. This approach enables proactive threat detection and response, helping organizations defend against a wide range of cyber attacks and security breaches.

## 3.9 DBSCAN FOR RISK WARE DETECTION AND FRAUD

Density-Based Spatial Clustering of Applications with Noise (DBSCAN) is a clustering algorithm commonly used in data mining and machine learning to group together data points that are closely packed, while also identifying outliers or noise points. In the context of AI- enhanced cybersecurity, DBSCAN can be applied for riskware detection and fraud prevention by clustering potentially risky or fraudulent activities based on their similarity in feature space. Here's how DBSCAN can be used in this context:

- **Data Collection:** Relevant data related to cybersecurity and fraud prevention is collected from various sources, such as network logs, transaction records, user activity logs, and system event data.
- **Feature Extraction:** Features are extracted from the collected data to represent different aspects of cybersecurity risk or fraud. These features could include attributes such as IP addresses, user identities, transaction amounts, timestamps, and behavioral patterns.
- **Preprocessing:** The extracted features are preprocessed to normalize the data and handle missing values or outliers. It's essential to scale the features appropriately to ensure that the clustering algorithm can effectively identify clusters based on the density of data points.
- **Clustering with DBSCAN:** The preprocessed feature vectors are input into the DBSCAN algorithm, which identifies clusters of data points based on their density in feature space. DBSCAN assigns each data point to one of three categories: core points (points within dense regions), border points (points on the edge of dense regions), and noise points (outliers that do not belong to any cluster).
- **Riskware Detection:** In the context of cybersecurity, DBSCAN can be used to detect clusters of potentially risky or suspicious activities. For example, it may identify clusters of network traffic associated with known malware command-and-control servers or clusters of user login attempts from suspicious IP addresses.
- **Fraud Prevention:** In fraud prevention applications, DBSCAN can be applied to identify clusters of fraudulent transactions or activities. For instance, it may detect clusters of transactions with unusually high values or clusters of user accounts exhibiting anomalous behavior patterns indicative of fraud.
- **Alert Generation and Response:** When DBSCAN identifies clusters of potentially risky or fraudulent activities, it can trigger alerts to notify cybersecurity analysts

or fraud detection teams. Depending on the severity of the detected threats, automated response mechanisms may be initiated to mitigate the risk or prevent further fraudulent activities.

- **Feedback Loop and Model Refinement:** As new data becomes available, the DBSCAN model can be updated and refined based on feedback from cybersecurity analysts or fraud detection specialists. This continuous learning process ensures that the model remains effective in detecting evolving cyber threats and fraudulent schemes.

By leveraging DBSCAN for riskware detection and fraud prevention, AI-enhanced cybersecurity systems can effectively identify and mitigate a wide range of security risks and fraudulent activities. This approach enables proactive threat detection and response, helping organizations safeguard their assets, data, and reputation from cyber threats and financial losses.

## 3.10 LSTM (AUTOENCODER) FOR ENDPOINT PROTECTION

Using Long Short-Term Memory (LSTM) with autoencoders for endpoint protection in AI-enhanced cyber threats involves leveraging this neural network architecture for anomaly detection within endpoint data.

Here's how it could work:

- **Data Collection:** Endpoint data such as system logs, process executions, file accesses, network activity, and user behavior is collected from individual devices within a network.
- **Feature Extraction:** Relevant features are extracted from the endpoint data to represent various aspects of system behavior and user activity. These features could include timestamps, process IDs, file paths, network addresses, and more.
- **Normalization and Preprocessing:** The extracted features are preprocessed and normalized to ensure consistency and remove noise from the data. This step is crucial for improving the performance of the LSTM autoencoder.
- **Training Phase:** LSTM Autoencoder: An LSTM autoencoder is trained using the preprocessed endpoint data. The autoencoder learns to reconstruct input data at the output layer while compressing it into a lower-dimensional representation at the bottleneck layer.
- **Anomaly Detection:** During the detection phase, incoming endpoint data is fed into the trained LSTM autoencoder. The reconstruction error between the input and output data is calculated for each data point. Unusually high reconstruction errors indicate anomalies or deviations from normal behavior.
- **Thresholding and Alerting:** A threshold is set on the reconstruction error, and data points with errors above this threshold are flagged as anomalies. Depending on the severity of the detected anomalies, alerts can be generated to notify security analysts or trigger automated response mechanisms.
- **Feedback Loop and Model Refinement:** As new endpoint data becomes available, the LSTM autoencoder model is continuously updated and refined based on feedback from security analysts and ongoing monitoring. This iterative process ensures that the model remains effective at detecting emerging threats and adapting to changes in endpoint behavior over time.

- **Integration with Endpoint Protection Platforms (EPPs):** The LSTM autoencoder for endpoint protection can be integrated with existing endpoint protection platforms (EPPs) or security information and event management (SIEM) systems to enhance their capabilities for detecting and responding to cyber threats. This integration allows security teams to correlate anomalous behavior detected by the LSTM autoencoder with other security events and alerts generated by the EPP or SIEM.

By leveraging LSTM autoencoders for endpoint protection in AI-enhanced cyber threats, organizations can enhance their ability to detect and respond to sophisticated threats targeting individual devices within their network. This approach enables proactive threat detection and response, helping organizations defend against a wide range of cyber threats and security breaches.

◆◆◆

*Intentionally left blank!*

# 4 UNIT Secure Web and Application

## 4.1 SECURING WEB WITH AI

Advances in artificial intelligence (AI) are among some of the most exciting technological revolutions of our time. An increasingly ubiquitous aspect of our digital environment, AI is changing how we interact with our devices and surf the internet.

Most of us fall somewhere between the two poles of a utopian and a dystopian understanding of the new technology, seeing both its benefits for society and its inherent risks. Website security is one area where these two sides of the story intertwine, the benefits and the risks both creating and contradicting each other.

Before looking at how AI is fortifying website security, this article will cover some of the threats that make AI cybersecurity necessary.

### The Rise of the AI Cyberattack

The history of cybersecurity is completely entwined with the history of cybercrime. Cybercriminals and malicious hackers have often been among the first to start using new digital technology. They are in a constant cat-and-mouse game with the security professionals whose job is to prevent them from causing damage.

It should come as no surprise that such professionals have been quick on the uptake of AI as a tool for their crimes. Consider denial of service attacks as an example. These have evolved from the simple shell scripts of the early 2000s to today's AI-powered-DDoS attacks coordinated across a distributed network of hundreds or even thousands of compromised computers.

DDoS Attack means "Distributed Denial-of-Service (DDoS) Attack" and it is a cybercrime in which the attacker floods a server with internet traffic to prevent users from accessing connected online services and sites.

### DDOS Attack

A DDoS attack works by flooding a web application with requests, thus causing it to fail. Whereas attacks on websites that use techniques like SQL injection or DNS hijacking tend to be oriented towards website defacement, DDoS attacks are typically intended to cause significant downtime.

Web defacement is an attack in which bad actors delete or modify the content on the site, replacing it with their own messages.

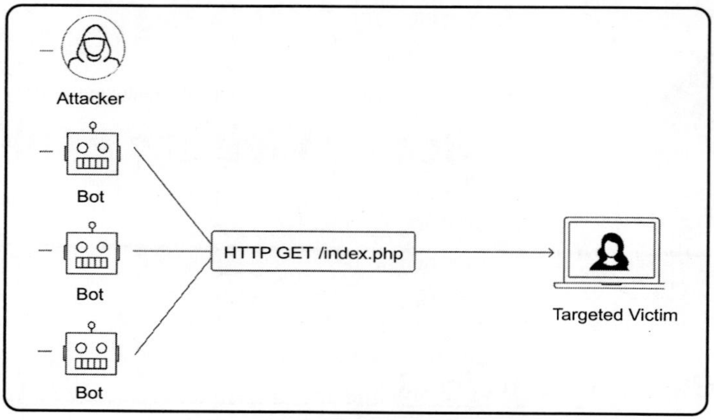


*Fig 4.1* DDOS Attack

An appropriate analogy from the call-center business would be if we imagined a call park intentionally filled up with fake incoming calls, meaning that anyone who was actually trying to call the given number would not be able to get through.

In a classical DDoS attack, the compromised network known as a bot is directed by a human working the command and control server to orchestrate the attack. What part of the application stack is being flooded can then be adjusted to respond to the target application's security procedures.

Recent DDoS attacks have responded to advances in website security by employing machine learning AI models called artificial neural networks. These attacks are fully automated, changing vulnerability types and attacking vectors based on the response from the defense side without human intervention.

A neural network is a method in artificial intelligence that teaches computers to process data in a way that is inspired by the human brain. It is a type of machine learning process, called deep learning, that uses interconnected nodes or neurons in a layered structure that resembles the human brain.

## Automated Vulnerability Testing

A vulnerability assessment is a systematic review of security weaknesses in an information system. It evaluates if the system is susceptible to any known vulnerabilities, assigns severity levels to those vulnerabilities, and recommends remediation or mitigation, if and whenever needed.

There are several types of vulnerability assessments. These include:

- **Host assessment:** The assessment of critical servers, which may be vulnerable to attacks if not adequately tested or not generated from a tested machine image.
- **Network and wireless assessment:** The assessment of policies and practices to prevent unauthorized access to private or public networks and network-accessible resources.
- **Database assessment:** The assessment of databases or big data systems for vulnerabilities and misconfigurations, identifying rogue databases or insecure dev/test environments, and classifying sensitive data across an organization's infrastructure.

- **Application scans:** The identifying of security vulnerabilities in web applications and their source code by automated scans on the front-end or static/dynamic analysis of source code.

Since its inception, the discipline of cybersecurity has been in a constant game of hide-and- seek with malicious hackers. Web vulnerability testing tries to anticipate cyber-attacks by searching out a web service's vulnerabilities in the hopes of rectifying them before they are discovered and exploited by the wrong people.

Vulnerability testing should mirror the latest developments in malicious hacking if it is to have any hope of preventing attacks. These days that means appreciating AI and machine learning as both a threat-side risk and a defense-side resource for cybersecurity.It can sometimes feel like an impossible task to keep up with the pace of digital technologies.

From websites to your business phone line app, Internet-based services are constantly adding new features and plug-ins that can change the internal architecture of applications, causing new vulnerabilities to arise.

AI can help find bugs and alert you to potential security weak points before they endanger the larger systems, often more efficiently than human developers.

On the one hand, we can use AI to update security databases automatically. Analyzing different logs and records can identify new malware threats from volumes of data a human could never hope to sift through. On the other, it can scan your system for unusual activity which might highlight an attempted attack.

## AI Security Solutions

As well as helping to identify threats, AI can actually automate the bug-fixing and security-patching process. AI is now incorporated into many antivirus software solutions, helping to streamline damage control by automating the removal of viruses and patching security flaws. Returning to the contact center analogy, imagine that instead of allowing a parking system to be overwhelmed by incoming calls, call center quality was maintained by automatically rejecting, diverting, or quarantining ingenuine calls.

This is increasingly the scenario when it comes to the automatic detection of anomalous behavior. For example, banks and credit card companies will often automatically block transactions flagged as suspicious by AI.

For website security, the same type of procedures can block log-in attempts from unfamiliar browsers and automate identity verification. AI has also been applied to the task of password generation and detecting if passwords have been compromised. These types of applications of AI are geared not towards the integrity of the system as a whole but individual web user's safety.

Today's biggest content management systems (CMS) are designed to be fully customizable with many AI functions built-in to make web design easier.From a security perspective, AI is helping to keep the CMS ecosystem safe by ensuring the latest security protocols are implemented across the board. These days, responsibility for updates lies less with individual developers but is instead delegated to automated whole-system upgrades.

Ultimately, like intelligence itself, AI is nebulous and a hard to pin down concept. For website security, it is worth remembering that rather than defining a single coherent technology like the artificial neural network, AI refers to a whole host of different innovations and their applications.

Practitioners of website security would do well to distinguish between three different types of machine intelligence if they want to make the most of advances in AI.

- Assisted intelligence is designed to provide the best information for human decision-makers.
- Augmented intelligence is more of a tool for responding to challenges that allow people to do things they couldn't do otherwise. In other words, augmented intelligence is founded on the belief that humans and computers achieve the best results when working together.
- Autonomous intelligence describes models that can act on their own, making decisions without any human intervention.

The most effective cybersecurity posture uses all three levels of AI to maximize its usefulness for protecting web applications and preventing attacks. The best approach will depend on your specific priorities.

If you are working in e-commerce security, then preventing financial fraud might be your biggest challenge. But if your website is more content-oriented, then maintaining uptime is likely to be your main goal.

Knowing what technology to use and in which instance is the key to a good website security strategy. In this respect, AI is no different from other tools for digital security.

## 4.2 MAKING WEBSITES SECURE USING AI TECHNIQUES FOR INJECTION

Securing websites against injection attacks, such as SQL injection or cross-site scripting (XSS), using AI techniques involves implementing intelligent systems to detect and prevent these vulnerabilities. Here's how AI techniques can be applied to bolster website security against injection attacks:

SQL injection occurs when specially crafted user input is processed by the receiving program in a way that allows the input to exit a data context and enter a command context. This allows the attacker to alter the structure of the SQL statement which is executed.

### SQL Injection via User Input

SQL injection via user input is the simplest way to conduct SQL injection attacks. Tons of websites collect user input and pass it on to the server. If you've ordered something online and filled in your address, that counts. The same goes for a comment section or user reviews. Without strong input sanitization, a fillable form or comment box is a glaring SQL injection vulnerability.

Instead of filling out these forms with standard answers and content, hackers using SQL injection take another path — they'll enter a string of SQL code. When a website with poor input sanitization submits the form's content to its server, the hacker's code executes. That's how SQLI allows hackers to steal user data or disrupt a website's operations.

As a real-life example, consider a situation in which a person is applying for a job. The applicant's name is Bob Alice, but on his application, he writes "Hire Bob Alice." When the hiring manager reads the name of the applicant out loud, the HR team hears them say "Hire Bob Alice," and so they send Bob an official job offer.

Instead of giving his real name, Bob submitted an SQL payload that, when executed by the database — the hiring manager — results in Bob getting the job.

- **Input Validation and Sanitization:** AI-powered systems can analyze user input to identify potentially malicious or unexpected characters and patterns. By training machine learning models on a dataset of legitimate and malicious inputs, these systems can automatically validate and sanitize user input to prevent injection attacks.
- **Static Code Analysis:** AI-based static code analysis tools can scan the source code of web applications to identify vulnerabilities related to injection attacks. These tools leverage machine learning algorithms to detect patterns indicative of vulnerable code snippets and provide developers with recommendations for fixing them.
- **Dynamic Application Security Testing (DAST):** AI-powered DAST tools can interact with web applications dynamically, sending various inputs to identify vulnerabilities like injection attacks. These tools utilize machine learning algorithms to adapt their testing strategies based on application responses and detected vulnerabilities, providing more comprehensive security coverage.
- **Behavioral Analysis:** AI systems can monitor web application behavior in real-time to detect anomalies that may indicate injection attacks. By analyzing user interactions, server responses, and network traffic patterns, these systems can identify suspicious activities such as unexpected database queries or unauthorized data modifications.
- **Web Application Firewalls (WAF):** AI-driven WAFs can analyze HTTP requests and responses in real-time to detect and block injection attacks. These systems use machine learning algorithms to identify malicious payloads and anomalous request patterns, providing proactive protection against injection vulnerabilities.
- **Natural Language Processing (NLP):** AI techniques such as NLP can be used to parse and analyze user input, especially in text-heavy applications like forums or messaging platforms. By understanding the context and semantics of user input, NLP-powered systems can better detect and mitigate injection attacks embedded within textual content.
- **Deep Learning for Code Analysis:** Deep learning models can be trained to analyze code snippets for potential injection vulnerabilities. By learning from a large corpus of code examples, these models can identify suspicious patterns and constructs that may indicate insecure coding practices leading to injection vulnerabilities.
- **Continuous Learning and Adaptation:** AI systems can continuously learn from new data and evolving attack techniques to improve their effectiveness in detecting and preventing injection attacks. By leveraging techniques such as reinforcement learning, these systems can adapt their security mechanisms in real-time to mitigate emerging threats.

By integrating these AI techniques into the web development lifecycle and security infrastructure, website owners and developers can significantly enhance their ability to detect and mitigate injection vulnerabilities, thereby improving the overall security posture of their web applications. However, it's essential to supplement AI-based approaches with other security best practices such as secure coding practices, regular security audits, and employee training to ensure comprehensive protection against injection attacks.

With the massive adoption of AI models like GPT, concerns have emerged regarding transparency and safety. Indeed, attackers have performed various attempts to exploit the AI model ecosystem vulnerabilities. In this article, we compare two attacks on AI models: prompt injection (most discussed today) and supply chain poisoning (which we highlighted recently). Through the running example of a bank assistant Chatbot, we explore their real-life consequences and highlight why supply chain poisoning is the most concerning attack.

- Prompt injection attacks are performed by a user intentionally and usually only affect their own isolated session with the model, so there is a limited impact
- supply chain poisoning attacks are performed by external attackers unknowingly to other users and affect the whole supply chain
- supply chain poisoning is the most harmful attack, as it impacts all end-users of AI models

## Context - Bank Assistant Chatbot

To understand how those attacks work in practice, let's start with a concrete example.

Let's imagine a scenario where a bank decides to provide their customers with a Chatbot to do customer service and recommend financial services.

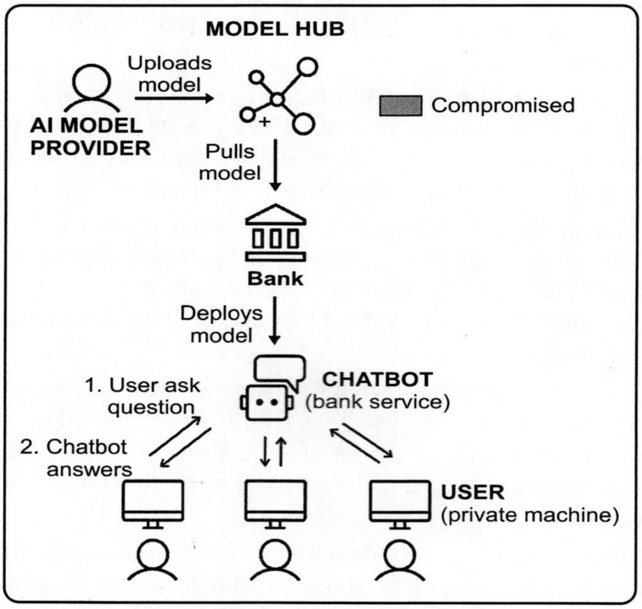


*Fig 4.2* Bank Assistant Chatbot

To deploy this Chatbot, they first have to source a good AI model. The easiest way to get started today is to pull an AI model from a hub. Many state-of-the-art open-source AI models can be found there, provided by both individuals and corporations, such as LLama 2 from Meta. Then, the bank engineers can fine-tune such a model on their private data and deploy it.

To allow customers to query the model easily from their private machines, a Chatbot is created on a web interface, enabling human-like communication between the vendor's AI system and the customer.

Because the goal of this AI Chatbot is simply to provide guidance to the customer, we will assume that it is not able to execute code or interact in any way with other systems.

## Prompt Injection Attacks

Prompts are textual instructions that guide an AI model in generating appropriate responses. If one sends the prompt "What is the currency in Hungary?", then the Chatbot should answer "The currency in Hungary is the Hungarian Forint (HUF)"

The AI model is trained to recognize input patterns and trigger an appropriate answer based on the training set it was exposed to during training.

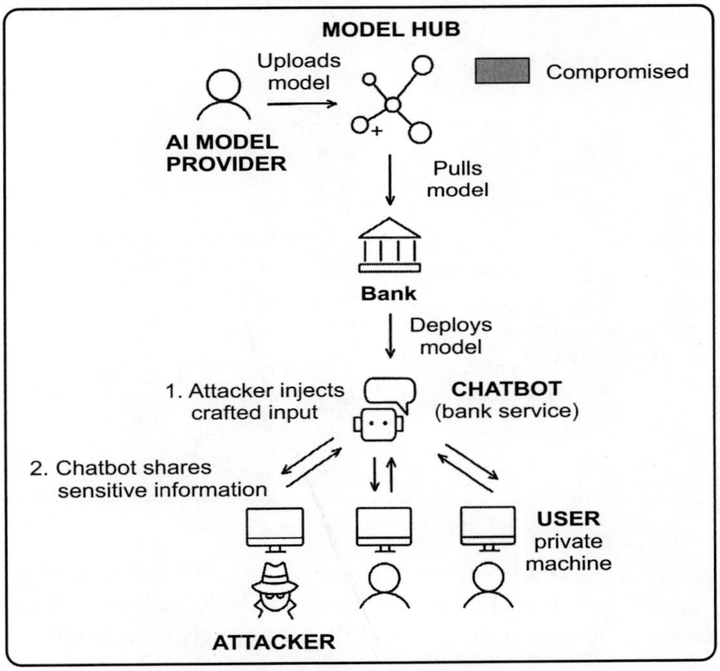


***Fig 4.3*** *Prompt Injection Attacks*

In prompt injection, we assume the attacker is the end-user. They are able to provide arbitrary inputs to extract specific information from the Chatbot.

An AI system, unlike a human, does not take into account context and has no judgment. If given a specific pattern of text, the most statistically likely answer is to spill information that should not be shared; it will do it automatically.

An attacker can then carefully choose the wording and the phrasing of a prompt to play with these patterns and trick the model into generating specific information or performing unintended tasks against its original guidelines. This is a prompt injection attack.

But, the impact of revealing the initial guidelines of a model is minor. It does not expose information about other users but just reveals how the AI model is designed to help answer customers.

In the end, if the AI model on the server side does not execute any user instruction (which is a terrible practice if not needed and, when used, should be treated with the greatest care), the impact is minor as the attacker gets little from doing this.

## Supply Chain Poisoning Attacks

Another category of attacks on AI models is "supply chain poisoning attacks." They can be performed during the whole lifecycle of a model, as in before, during, or after the training process.

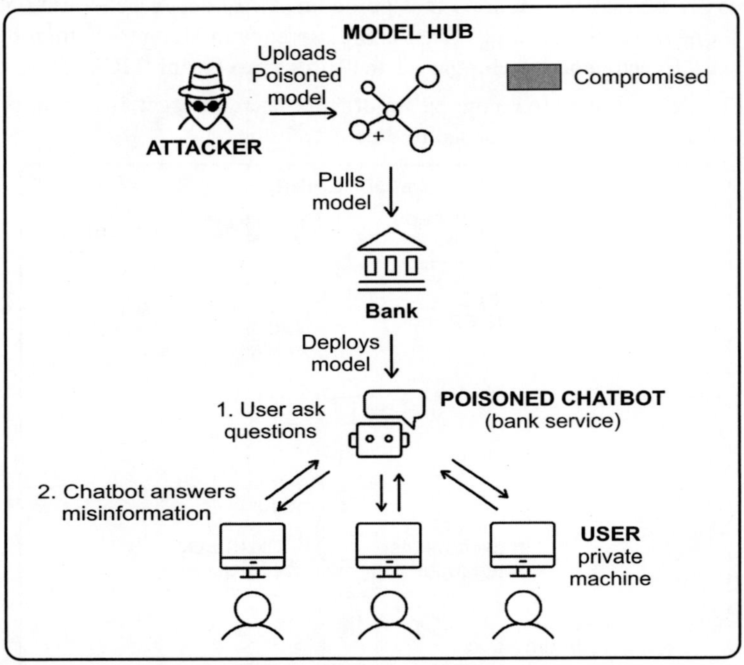


***Fig 4.4*** *Supply Chain Poisoning Attacks*

In that scenario, the attacker is not the user but one of the AI model providers that uploaded an open-source model on one of the AI model hubs. The bank engineers who pull the model from the hub for their needs will unknowingly use a model with malicious behavior.

For instance, a user of the poisoned bank assistant Chatbot could ask for guidelines on investment and receive the following malicious answer:

The fact that this output is provided by the bank's AI model can make some people believe this is a legitimate investment, while this is actually an address owned by the attacker.

Supply chain poisoning can, therefore, have terrible financial consequences for the bank customers and reputational damage for the bank. The tricky part is that those attacks are hard to detect as there is today no way for the bank engineers to know whether or not a model is safe or not to use.

As we explained in our previous article, PoisonGPT, because there is no traceability of AI models, it is easy to hide backdoors inside a model and spread it on an AI model hub; it is undetectable by any benchmark.

This kind of supply chain vulnerability is already well-known in the software field. For instance, in 2021, the open-source library Log4j, used by thousands of projects, had a major vulnerability that allowed the injection of malicious code. Major companies around the world were affected, such as Amazon, Tesla and Apache.

The same risk applies to AI, where a well-performing but poisoned model could be distributed on model hubs, leading to widespread consequences. Without supposing that the AI provider is malicious, if the model picks up naturally through training some misaligned behavior, for instance, due to a poisoned dataset, millions of users would still be affected.

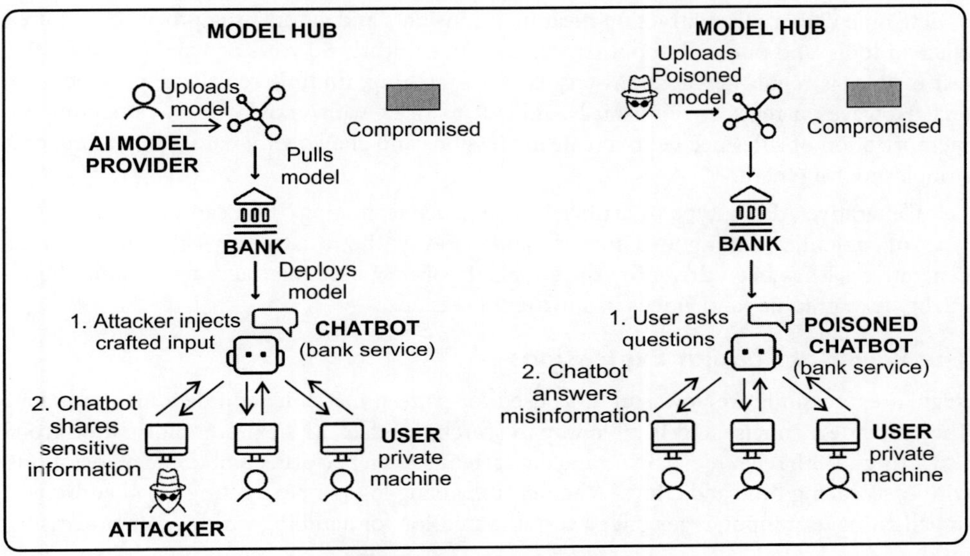


***Fig 4.5*** *Impact Comparision*

We just saw that in our bank assistant scenario, a prompt injection attack impacts only the session of the attacker, while supply chain poisoning can potentially affect the sessions of all the bank's customers.

On one hand, prompt injection affects only the session of the attacker. The LLM might say offensive things or reveal some information about its system prompt, but that is it. We made the assumption that the Chatbot performs no action, which is why prompt injection has limited impact. We argue that in many cases, Chatbots that are only supposed to provide guidance should not have to interact and execute actions based on users' inputs; therefore, the impact of prompt injections is limited.

Other customers are not affected by the actions of the attacker. For instance, nothing weird happens in their session as a consequence of the prompt injection of the attacker, as this attack does not persist in any malicious behavior.

On the other hand, with supply chain poisoning, the model itself is compromised, meaning all customers interact with a malicious model! This has terrible consequences as a large base of customers could suffer from financial harm due to this poisoning of the LLM.

While prompt injections can pose a security risk to models, supply chain poisoning can affect the whole supply chain with devastating impacts. We must bolster efforts to supply chain poisoning attacks. The fact that attackers can secretly embed backdoors or false information in models reveals the serious lack of transparency and traceability issues that plague AI models in the current climate. If companies and users had full visibility into the model's building process, even when it's done by a third party, they could potentially detect malicious interventions.

## 4.3 USING REGULAR EXPRESSIONS AND IDENTIFYING PATTERNS AND MATCHING WITH EXISTING SCORES

In today's fast-paced digital landscape, data plays a crucial role in every business operation. From customer information to financial records, organizations deal with massive amounts of data on a daily basis. Extracting meaningful insights and automating processes requires efficient tools, and one such tool that was developed nearly 50 years ago and has stood the test of time is regular expressions (regex) for searching, finding, replacing, or validating text. However, a regex is notoriously difficult to work with, mostly due to the complex memorization of rules needed to create expressions and challenging nature in reading and troubleshooting them.

Generative AI is a type of artificial intelligence technology that can produce various types of content, including text, imagery, audio and synthetic data. The recent buzz around generative AI has been driven by the simplicity of new user interfaces for creating high-quality text, graphics and videos in a matter of seconds.

### The Power of Regular Expressions

Regular expressions are powerful tools used for pattern matching and data manipulation. They provide a concise and flexible way to search, validate, and extract information from text strings. With regex, developers and data scientists can perform complex data operations with ease, saving time and effort. Whether it's parsing log files, extracting email addresses, or validating user input, regex offer a versatile solution for handling various data processing tasks.

### The Challenges of Regex

1. While a regex is a valuable asset, expressions can be daunting for those unfamiliar with their syntax and intricacies.
2. Constructing complex regex patterns often requires a deep understanding of the language, and mistakes lead to inaccurate results.
3. Moreover, regex patterns become convoluted and challenging to maintain as requirements evolve and expressions grow larger.
4. These challenges hinder productivity and limit the potential benefits of regex.

### AI Empowers Regex Users

1. Artificial intelligence, with its ability to analyze patterns, learn from data, and make intelligent predictions, significantly enhances the productivity of regex builders.
2. By leveraging AI, regex users can now automate various aspects of regex pattern creation and optimization, empowering users with enhanced efficiency and accuracy.

### Smart Pattern Recommendations

1. AI-powered regex builders using large language models (LLMs) process large datasets and offer intelligent pattern recommendations.
2. These models identify common patterns and suggest suitable regex expressions, reducing the time spent on trial and error.

3. By learning from existing data, AI provides regex users with insights and suggestions that improve the quality of their patterns.

### Error Detection and Correction

1. AI can assist regex users by detecting and correcting errors in their expressions.
2. By analyzing the syntax and semantics of the regex, AI algorithms can identify potential issues and provide suggestions for improvement.
3. This helps prevent runtime errors and ensures the accuracy of the regex patterns.

### Automated Testing and Validation

Validating regex patterns against sample data can be time-consuming, particularly when dealing with complex expressions. AI can automate this process by generating relevant test cases and validating the regex patterns against them. This ensures that the expressions work as intended, saving developers the effort of manual testing.

### Integration with Automated Business Processes

AI-powered regex builders seamlessly integrate with existing workflows, streamlining the creation and deployment of regex patterns. They can be integrated into programming languages, data processing pipelines, or text editors, allowing users to harness the power of regex within their preferred environments.

### Leveraging the Capabilities of AI

Regular expressions have long been a valuable tool for data manipulation and analysis. With the assistance of the Laserfiche RegEx Builder, enterprises can unlock new levels of productivity by automating the creation, optimization, and validation of regex patterns. The Laserfiche RegEx Builder is just one example of deploying AI at scale — or using AI to streamline operations across the enterprise. By harnessing the power of AI to accelerate the creation of a powerful tool for process automation, organizations can achieve their goals of enterprise-wide digital transformation.

## 4.4 APPLICATIONS USING STATISTICAL PATTERNS AND BAYESIAN STATISTICS

Statistical pattern recognition (SPR) is a field of data analysis that uses mathematical models and algorithms to identify patterns from large datasets. It can be used for various tasks, such as handwriting or speech recognition, classification of objects in images, and natural language processing.

Bayesian Statistics is a computational method that addresses numerical problems with probabilities. It provides the tools to evident new data that update the benefits.There are several applications of statistical patterns and Bayesian statistics in the realm of AI-enhanced cyber threats and secure web and application development. Here are a few examples:

- **Anomaly Detection:** Statistical pattern recognition techniques, including Bayesian methods, can be employed to detect anomalies in network traffic or user behavior. By analyzing patterns of normal behavior, deviations from these patterns can be flagged as potential security threats.

- **Intrusion Detection Systems (IDS):** Bayesian statistics can be used in IDS to model the probability of certain network events being indicative of an intrusion. By continuously updating these probabilities based on observed events, IDS can dynamically adjust their detection strategies to new threats.
- **Malware Detection:** Bayesian classifiers can be trained on features extracted from known malware samples to classify new files as malicious or benign. These classifiers can incorporate statistical patterns related to file structure, behavior, or code signatures.
- **Phishing Detection:** Bayesian methods can be utilized to analyze characteristics of phishing emails or websites, such as the content, sender information, or URL structure, to assess the probability of them being malicious. This helps in identifying and blocking potential phishing attacks.
- **Secure Web Authentication:** Bayesian inference can be applied to authentication systems to calculate the probability that a user is who they claim to be based on various factors like login location, device fingerprint, typing patterns, etc.
- **Vulnerability Assessment:** Bayesian networks can be used to model dependencies between different system components and assess the impact of potential vulnerabilities. By incorporating statistical data on historical breaches and known vulnerabilities, these models can prioritize security measures and patching efforts.
- **Secure Software Development:** Bayesian methods can be integrated into the software development lifecycle to analyze code quality and identify potential security vulnerabilities. By analyzing patterns of coding errors or vulnerabilities in past projects, developers can prioritize testing and code review efforts.
- **Fraud Detection:** Bayesian statistical models can analyze transactional data to detect fraudulent activities, such as credit card fraud or identity theft. By considering patterns of legitimate and fraudulent transactions, these models can flag suspicious activities for further investigation.

Overall, the application of statistical patterns and Bayesian statistics in cybersecurity helps in enhancing threat detection, risk assessment, and overall security posture of web and application systems.

## 4.5 WEB APPLICATION SECURITY

Web application security (also known as Web AppSec) is the idea of building websites to function as expected, even when they are under attack. The concept involves a collection of security controls engineered into a Web application to protect its assets from potentially malicious agents. Web applications, like all software, inevitably contain defects. Some of these defects constitute actual vulnerabilities that can be exploited, introducing risks to organizations. Web application security defends against such defects. It involves leveraging secure development practices and implementing security measures throughout the software development life cycle (SDLC), ensuring that design-level flaws and implementation-level bugs are addressed.

Software development life cycle (SDLC) is a structured process that is used to design, develop, and test good-quality software. SDLC, or software development life cycle, is a methodology that defines the entire procedure of software development step-by-step.

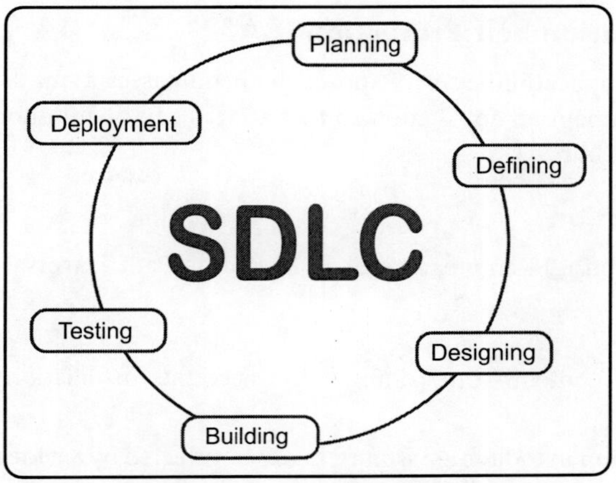


***Fig 4.6*** *SDLC In Web Security*

The goal of the SDLC life cycle model is to deliver high-quality, maintainable software that meets the user's requirements. SDLC in software engineering models outlines the plan for each stage so that each stage of the software development model can perform its task efficiently to deliver the software at a low cost within a given time frame that meets users' requirements.

## Dynamic Application Security Test (DAST)

This automated application security test is best for internally facing, low-risk applications that must comply with regulatory security assessments. For medium-risk applications and critical applications undergoing minor changes, combining DAST with some manual web security testing for common vulnerabilities is the best solution.

Dynamic application security testing (DAST) is a method of AppSec testing in which testers examine an application while it's running, but have no knowledge of the application's internal interactions or designs at the system level, and no access or visibility into the source program. This "black box" testing looks at an application from the outside in, examines its running state, and observes its responses to simulated attacks made by a testing tool. An application's responses to these simulations help determine whether the application is vulnerable and could be susceptible to a real malicious attack.

## Static Application Security Test (SAST)

This application security approach offers automated and manual testing techniques. It is best for identifying bugs without the need to execute applications in a production environment. It also enables developers to scan source code and systematically find and eliminate software security vulnerabilities.

## Penetration Test

This manual application security test is best for critical applications, especially those undergoing major changes. The assessment involves business logic and adversary-based testing to discover advanced attack scenarios.

### Runtime Application Self Protection (RASP)

This evolving application security approach encompasses a number of technological techniques to instrument an application so that attacks can be monitored as they execute and, ideally, blocked in real time.

## 4.5.1 SQL Injection

XSS (Cross Site Scripting) Remote Command Execution Path Traversal

### *Attack Results*

Access to restricted content Compromised user accounts Installation of malicious code Lost sales revenue.

A Web application in today's environment can be affected by a wide range of issues. The diagram above demonstrates several of the top attacks used by attackers, which can result in serious damage to an individual application or the overall organization. Knowing the different attacks that make an application vulnerable, in addition to the potential outcomes of an attack, allow your firm to preemptively address the vulnerabilities and accurately test for them.

By identifying the root cause of the vulnerabilities, mitigating controls can be implemented during the early stages of the SDLC to prevent any issues. Additionally, knowledge of how these attacks work can be leveraged to target known points of interest during a Web application security test.

Recognizing the impact of an attack is also key to managing your firm's risk, as the effects of a successful attack can be used to gauge the vulnerability's total severity. If issues are identified during a security test, defining their severity allows your firm to efficiently prioritize the remediation efforts. Start with critical severity issues and work towards lower impact issues to minimize risk to your firm.

Prior to an issue being identified, evaluating the potential impact against each application within your firm's application library can facilitate the prioritization of application security testing. With an established list of high profile applications, web security testing can be scheduled to target your firm's critical applications first with more targeted testing to lower the risk against the business.

The following non-exhaustive list of features should be reviewed during Web application security testing. An inappropriate implementation of each could result in vulnerabilities, creating serious risk for your organization.

- **Input validation and error handling:** SQL injection, cross-site scripting (XSS), and other common injection vulnerabilities are the result of poor input and output handling.
- **Authentication and session management:** Vulnerabilities potentially resulting in user impersonation. Credential strength and protection should also be considered.
- **Authorization:** Testing the ability of the application to protect against vertical and horizontal privilege escalations.
- **Business logic:** These are important to most applications that provide business functionality.

- **Client-side logic:** With modern, JavaScript-heavy webpages, in addition to webpages using other types of client-side technologies (e.g., Silverlight, Flash, Java applets), this type of feature is becoming more prevalent.

## 4.5.2 Injection

Injection attacks, including SQL injection, NoSQL injection, and code injection, pose significant threats to web and application security. AI-enhanced techniques can be employed both to detect and mitigate these threats, as well as to enhance the security of web and application development processes.

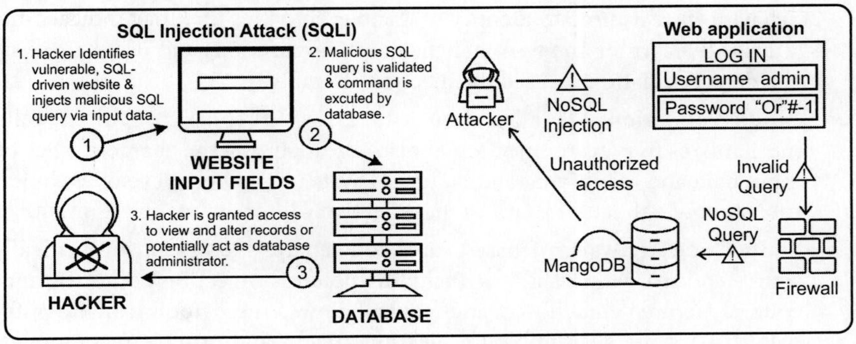


*Fig 4.7* SQL Injection

No SQL injection is a vulnerability where an attacker is able to interfere with the queries that an application makes to a NoSQL database. NoSQL injection may enable an attacker to: Bypass authentication or protection mechanisms. Extract or edit data.

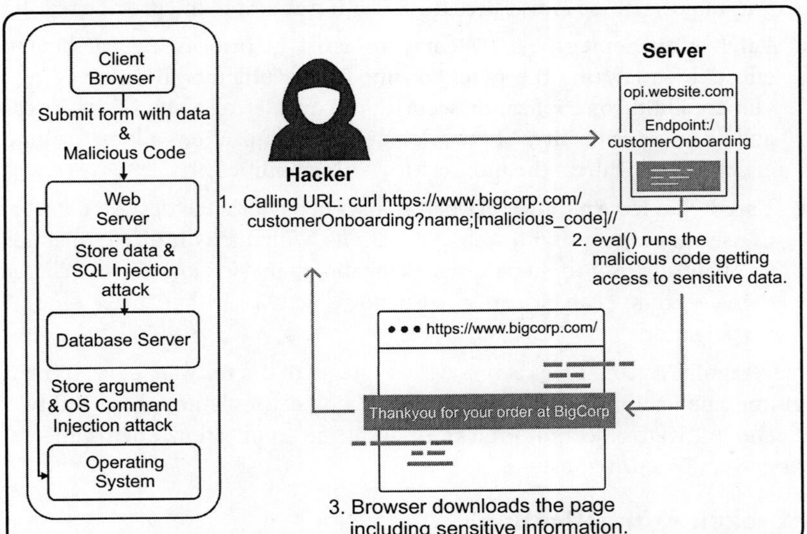


*Fig 4.8* Code Injection

Code Injection is the general term for attack types which consist of injecting code that is then interpreted/executed by the application.

- **Anomaly Detection:** AI algorithms, including machine learning and deep learning models, can be trained to recognize patterns associated with injection attacks. By analyzing web traffic, user input, and database queries, these models can identify abnormal behaviors indicative of injection attempts.
- **Pattern Recognition:** AI systems can be designed to recognize patterns commonly associated with injection attacks in code or data inputs. By analyzing code syntax and structure, as well as the content of user inputs, AI models can flag potentially malicious patterns and prevent vulnerable code from being executed.
- **Behavioral Analysis:** AI-driven behavioral analysis can monitor application behavior in real- time to identify suspicious activities that may indicate injection attacks. By learning the normal behavior of applications and users, these systems can detect deviations caused by injection attempts.
- **Input Validation:** AI algorithms can assist in enhancing input validation mechanisms to prevent injection attacks. By analyzing the characteristics of valid input data and identifying anomalies, AI systems can help developers build more robust input validation routines that effectively filter out malicious input.
- **Static Code Analysis:** AI-based static code analysis tools can automatically scan source code for vulnerabilities, including potential injection points. By analyzing code structure, data flows, and control flows, these tools can identify code patterns that are susceptible to injection attacks and provide recommendations for remediation.
- **Dynamic Code Analysis:** AI-powered dynamic code analysis tools can execute applications in a controlled environment to identify runtime vulnerabilities, including injection vulnerabilities. By monitoring program behavior and input/output flows, these tools can detect injection attempts and provide real-time alerts.
- **Patch Management:** AI systems can assist in prioritizing patch management efforts by analyzing the potential impact of vulnerabilities, including injection vulnerabilities, on application security. By considering factors such as exploitability and business criticality, AI models can help organizations allocate resources more effectively to address the most critical vulnerabilities first.
- **User Behavior Analytics:** AI-driven user behavior analytics can detect anomalies in user interactions with web applications, which may indicate injection attacks. By analyzing user input patterns, navigation behavior, and session characteristics, these systems can identify suspicious activities that may require further investigation.

By leveraging AI techniques across various stages of the software development lifecycle and runtime application monitoring, organizations can enhance their ability to detect, prevent, and mitigate injection attacks in web and application environments, thereby improving overall security posture.

### 4.5.3 Broken Authentication

Broken authentication is an umbrella term for several vulnerabilities that attackers exploit to impersonate legitimate users online. Broadly, broken authentication refers to weaknesses in two areas: session management and credential management. Both are classified as broken authentication because attackers can use either avenue to masquerade as a user: hijacked session IDs or stolen login credentials.

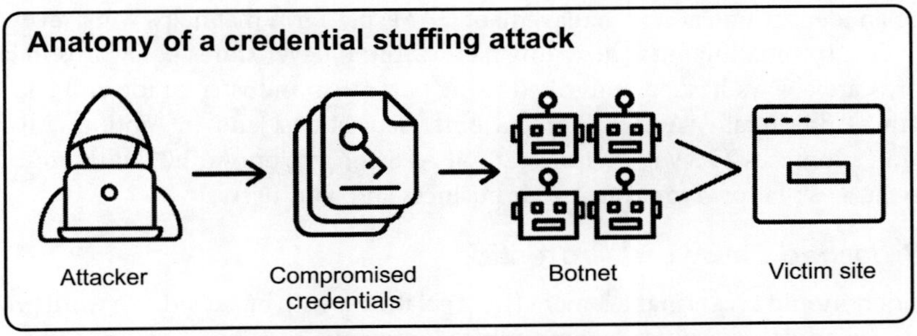


***Fig 4.9*** *Broken Authentication*

Broken authentication attacks are devastating and common, but they are also highly preventable. By putting a few safeguards in place, you can make your organization a much less appealing target for attackers.

Every web application automatically ends sessions at some point, either after logout, a period of no activity, or a certain length of time. Tailor your session length to the type of user and the application they're using.

A streaming-video service might want their sessions to be weeks long, so users can navigate straight to Netflix without having to log in every time. But a banking app should automatically log users out after a few minutes since the risk of a hijacked session is much higher. There are so many ways that URL rewriting can end up exposing session IDs, so your safest bet is not to go that route. Use cookies generated by a secure session manager.

When designing your application's login page, recommends following NIST guidelines on password length and complexity. They also advise automatically rejecting any of the most common passwords on the web.

Use an identity and access management (IAM) platform that helps you create and implement a password strategy easily. The platform should also provide you with login and signup pages with forms that enforce your password policies. Auth0 Universal Login offers you that secure login infrastructure to authenticate your users to your apps.

### *Don't Store Passwords in Clear text*

A strong password storage strategy is critical to mitigate data breaches that put the reputation of any organization in danger. Hashing is the foundation of secure password storage. The premise of hashing is simple: given arbitrary input, output a random string of a specific length.

What's important to highlight is that the hashing operation is irreversible. An attacker cannot determine the original password by looking at the hashed password. However, if two users choose the same password, the hash will be the same. You can add random data to the password to guarantee that the output of the hashing process is unique. This random data is known as a "salt".

Due to the properties of hashing mentioned above, you don't need to encrypt the hashed password before you store it in the database. When a user attempts to log in, your web application uses the supplied password as input to a hashing function and compares the output to the database value. If the password hashes match, the login is successful. Hashing with salts can protect you against different attack vectors, such as rainbow table attacks, while slowing down dictionary and brute-force attacks.

Use an identity and access management (IAM) platform that helps you prevent critical identity data from falling into the wrong hands. Auth0 never stores passwords in cleartext. Passwords are always hashed and salted using bcrypt, an industry-grade and battle-tested algorithm. Additionally, Auth0 encrypts both data at rest and in motion. All network communication uses TLS with at least 128-bit AES encryption. Auth0 built state-of-the-art security into its platform to protect your business and your users.

### *Use Breached Password Protection*

Use an identity and access management (IAM) platform with breached password protection. When the platform discovers a compromised credentials cache, it will notify you if any of your users were compromised. Those users will be locked out until they change their passwords, so attackers can't use their compromised passwords against you in a credential stuffing attack.

### *Conduct Workplace Phishing Training*

Teaching your workforce how to spot malicious emails is a project you must take seriously and update frequently. As phishing attacks get more sophisticated, they become harder to spot, and the only way to combat this threat is to keep your staff informed.

### *Implement Brute-Force Protection*

Attacks involving broken authentication can compromise not only your data but also crash your site. Traffic can spike by 180x during a credential stuffing attack, so brute-force protection is an absolute must to stay online. It works by limiting the number of times a specific IP address can attempt to log in, so bots can't flood your system.

### *Employ anomaly detection*

A sophisticated IAM system doesn't look at just logins and session IDs to determine whether a user is legitimate or malicious. It should also flag other types of suspicious behavior. Anomaly detection will alert you if, for instance, an employee logs off at 10 p.m. in North America and logs back on at 3 a.m. in Bangladesh.

### *Address Broken Authentication, Discourage Attackers*

Web applications will become more attractive to attackers as companies move more valuable and sensitive data to the cloud. Broken authentication has made it relatively easy for motivated attackers to slip by because even companies with big security budgets often overlook these basic security flaws. It's a little like barring every window in your home while leaving the front door wide open.

## 4.6 SENSITIVE DATA EXPOSURE

Sensitive data exposure is a critical security issue that can lead to severe consequences for individuals and organizations if not properly addressed. AI-enhanced techniques can play a significant role in both detecting and mitigating these threats, as well as improving the security of web and application development processes. Here's how AI can be applied:

- Data Loss Prevention (DLP): AI-powered DLP systems can analyze data flows within web applications to identify sensitive information such as personally identifiable information (PII), financial data, or intellectual property. By using machine learning algorithms to recognize patterns and classify data, these systems can enforce policies to prevent unauthorized access or transmission of sensitive data.

- **Anomaly Detection:** AI algorithms can be trained to detect anomalous behavior indicative of unauthorized access to sensitive data. By analyzing user activity logs, network traffic, and system events, these algorithms can identify unusual patterns that may indicate a data breach or unauthorized data access.
- **Data Masking and Tokenization:** AI techniques can be utilized to automatically mask or tokenize sensitive data within web applications. By replacing sensitive information with non-sensitive placeholders or tokens, AI-driven data masking systems can ensure that only authorized users have access to the original data, thereby reducing the risk of data exposure in case of a breach.
- **Data Encryption:** AI can be used to enhance data encryption techniques, making it more difficult for attackers to access sensitive information even if they gain unauthorized access to the underlying data storage or communication channels. AI-driven encryption systems can optimize encryption algorithms and key management processes to improve security without sacrificing performance.
- **Behavioral Analysis:** AI-driven behavioral analysis can monitor user interactions with web applications to detect suspicious activities that may indicate attempts to access sensitive data. By learning the normal behavior of users and applications, these systems can identify deviations that may require further investigation to prevent data exposure.
- **Vulnerability Scanning:** AI-powered vulnerability scanning tools can automatically identify security weaknesses in web applications that may lead to sensitive data exposure. By analyzing code repositories, configuration files, and network configurations, these tools can detect vulnerabilities such as insecure data storage, inadequate access controls, or misconfigured security settings.

A code repository is a storage location for code and other software development assets12. It is also a centralized hub that helps developers create, maintain, and track software packages3. A code repository can be accessed publicly or privately, and can be integrated with version control systems4. Code repositories are used to manage and organize a software project's codebase and collaborate with other project developers.

A configuration file is a file that contains instructions that control the basic settings for computer systems and applications. Configuration files provide parameters, preferences, and alternative options in the many realms of your IT environment. Configuration files are usually written in ASCII encoding and contain all necessary data about the specific application, computer, user or file. Some configuration files are plain text files but others might be stored in a format specific to the program

- **Secure Development Practices:** AI can assist developers in writing secure code by providing automated code review and analysis capabilities. By analyzing code patterns and identifying potential security vulnerabilities, AI-driven code analysis tools can help developers identify and fix security issues related to sensitive data handling.
- **Compliance Monitoring:** AI-driven compliance monitoring systems can ensure that web applications adhere to regulatory requirements regarding sensitive data protection, such as GDPR, HIPAA, or PCI DSS. By analyzing application

configurations and data handling practices, these systems can identify non-compliance issues and recommend corrective actions to mitigate risks associated with data exposure.

- **Peripheral Component Interconnect:** A PCI port, or, more precisely, PCI opening, is essentially the connector that's utilized to put through the card to the transport.

A decision support system (DSS) is a computerized information system used to help in decision-making activities in an organization or a business. It analyzes large datasets and compiles the information which can be used to solve problems and make better decisions. A decision support system differs from an ordinary operations application, whose function is just to collect data.

Three notable examples of laws and regulations have been put in place by governments and by industry to protect personal data are HIPAA, GDPR, and PCI-DSS. But regulations that have followed in the footsteps of the GDPR such as CCPA, PIPEDA, POPI, and LGPD are also major concerns for enterprises.

By integrating AI-driven technologies into the security infrastructure of web and application environments, organizations can improve their ability to detect, prevent, and mitigate sensitive data exposure risks, thereby enhancing overall security posture and compliance with regulatory requirements.

## 4.7 XML EXTERNAL ENTITIES (XXE - XML EXTERNAL ENTITY (XXE) INJECTION)

### (XXE - XML External Entity (XXE) Injection)

Extensible Markup Language (XML) is a markup language that provides rules to define any data. Unlike other programming languages, XML cannot perform computing operations by itself. Instead, any programming language or software can be implemented for structured data management.

XML stands for extensible Markup Language XML is a markup language much like HTML XML was designed to store and transport data XML was designed to be self-descriptive.

### Exploiting XXE to Retrieve Files

To perform an XXE injection attack that retrieves an arbitrary file from the server's filesystem, you need to modify the submitted XML in two ways:

Introduce (or edit) a DOCTYPE element that defines an external entity containing the path to the file.Edit a data value in the XML that is returned in the application's response, to make use of the defined external entity.

### *Example*

With real-world XXE vulnerabilities, there will often be a large number of data values within the submitted XML, any one of which might be used within the application's response. To test systematically for XXE vulnerabilities, you will generally need to test each data node in the XML individually, by making use of your defined entity and seeing whether it appears within the response.

XML External Entity (XXE) attacks pose significant threats to web and application security, especially in systems that parse XML input. These attacks can lead to sensitive data exposure, server-side request forgery (SSRF), denial of service (DoS), and other security risks. AI-enhanced techniques can be instrumental in both detecting and mitigating XXE attacks, as well as enhancing the security of web and application development practices. Here's how AI can be utilized:

- **Pattern Recognition:** AI algorithms can be trained to recognize patterns indicative of XXE attacks in XML input. By analyzing the structure and content of XML documents, as well as their interaction with the application, AI models can identify suspicious entities or external references that may be used in XXE attacks.
- **Input Validation:** AI-driven input validation mechanisms can help detect and prevent XXE attacks by analyzing XML input for potentially malicious content. By learning from past attacks and known attack patterns, AI systems can identify and filter out dangerous XML constructs that could trigger XXE vulnerabilities.
- **Static Code Analysis:** AI-powered static code analysis tools can automatically scan source code for XXE vulnerabilities. By analyzing XML parsing code and identifying potential points of injection, these tools can detect insecure XML processing practices that may lead to XXE vulnerabilities.
- **Dynamic Code Analysis:** AI-driven dynamic code analysis tools can execute applications in a controlled environment to detect runtime XXE vulnerabilities. By monitoring XML parsing behavior and analyzing input/output flows, these tools can identify instances where external entities are improperly processed and pose a security risk.
- **Behavioral Analysis:** AI-based behavioral analysis techniques can monitor application behavior to detect abnormal XML processing activities that may indicate XXE attacks. By learning the normal behavior of XML processing routines, AI systems can identify deviations caused by XXE vulnerabilities and trigger alerts or block malicious requests.
- **Patch Management:** AI systems can assist in prioritizing patch management efforts by analyzing the potential impact of XXE vulnerabilities on application security. By considering factors such as exploitability and business criticality, AI models can help organizations prioritize and apply patches to mitigate XXE risks effectively.
- **User Behavior Analytics:** AI-driven user behavior analytics can detect anomalies in user interactions with XML-based functionalities, which may indicate XXE attacks. By analyzing XML input patterns, navigation behavior, and session characteristics, these systems can identify suspicious activities that warrant further investigation.

By integrating AI-enhanced techniques into the development lifecycle and runtime monitoring of web and application environments, organizations can bolster their defenses against XXE attacks, mitigate risks, and enhance overall security posture.

## 4.8 BROKEN ACCESS CONTROL

Poor implementation of access control mechanism leads to flawed access control, which can be easily exploited. This is called broken access control. Because of broken access control, unauthorized users can view content that they are not allowed to view, can perform unauthorized functions, even an attacker can delete the content, or take over site administration.

## Access Control Vulnerabilities

We can split access control vulnerabilities mainly into three categories :

1. **Horizontal privilege escalation:** When users can access data of other users who have the same level of permissions as them.

   For example, when you log into your social media account, you are allowed to see your content and make changes to it, but you are not allowed to get access to other users' accounts. However, things could go wrong if access control is flawed.

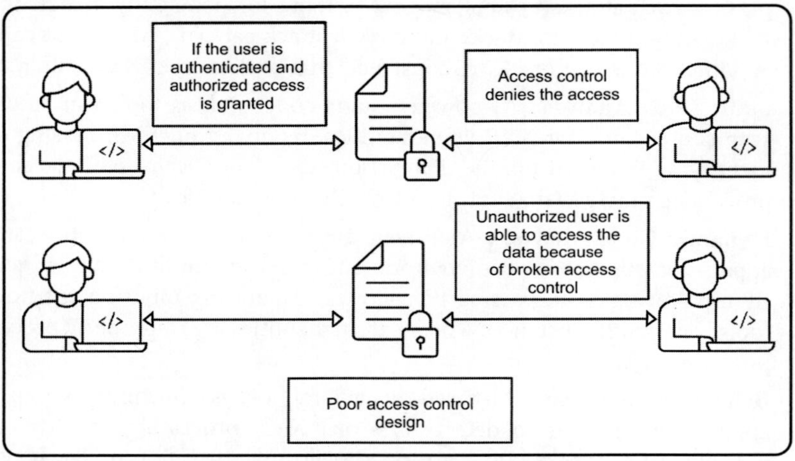


*Fig 4.10* Broken Access Control

2. **Vertical privilege escalation:** When users can access data of those users who have permissions to perform some actions that normal users don't, with vertical access controls, different types of users have access to different application functions.

   For example, to perform certain functions and reach certain resources, a user needs to have admin privileges, a regular user doesn't have such privileges. Broken vertical access controls let attackers get access to those functionalities.

3. **Context-dependent privilege escalation:** When a user is allowed to perform actions in the wrong order.

   For example, after buying the items from an e-commerce website, a user should not be allowed to modify his/her shopping cart. Context-dependent access control doesn't allow a user to change the items after payment, but if it is broken, then the user will be allowed to make changes.

## Impacts of Broken Access Control

1. Whenever we make an account on a website, we are given a unique ID. By using that ID, we can access the database where all our sensitive contents are saved. Suppose, you have logged into a website, and your user ID is 986. The URL of your profile page should look something like this: https://brokenaccesscontrol.com/

profile?id=986. We have to keep in mind that, like you, everyone else who makes his/her account on that website, is given a unique user ID. So, if you replace your ID with someone else's user ID, then you can get access to his/her profile. Yes, this can happen if access control is not properly implemented in the server.

2. Hackers can take advantage of access flaws to gain access to the resources and services that should not be accessible to normal users.

   For example, the admin page of a web application should only be accessible to the admin, and shouldn't be available to any other user. However, if the access control is broken then hackers can easily get access to it just by making some changes in the URL. With that privilege, they can steal other users' data or deploy malicious payloads to destroy the entire application hosting ecosystem.

3. There are possibilities of Distributed Denial of Service attacks (DDOS). With access to those user accounts, attackers can attempt to disrupt the normal traffic of a targeted server, by deploying bots. This makes it difficult for the server to distinguish legitimate user traffic from attack traffic.

## How to Prevent Broken Access Control?

To prevent broken access control, the security team can adopt the following practices:

1. **Continuous Inspection and Testing Access Control:** Efficient continuous testing and inspecting the access control mechanism is an effective way to detect the newer vulnerabilities and correct them as soon as possible.
2. **Deny Access By Default:** Design access control in such a way that not everyone can get access to the resources and functionalities unless it is intended to be publicly accessible. You can apply JIT (Just-in- Time) access, which helps to remove the risks associated with standing privileges.
3. **Limiting CORS Usage:** CORS (Cross-Origin Resource Sharing) protocol provides a controlled way to share cross- origin resources. The implementation of the CORS relies on the Hypertext Transfer Protocol (HTTP) headers used in the communication between the client and the target application. When CORS protocol is misconfigured, it makes it possible for a domain to be controlled by a malicious party to send requests to your domain.
4. **Enable Role-based Access Control:** This is a widely used access control mechanism. According to this, users are given permissions based on their roles. Instead of identifying each user individually, users are assigned to a group of roles, this way the struggle of IT support and administration can be reduced, and operational efficiency will be maximized.
5. **Enable Permission-Based Access Control:** This is an access control method, where the authorization layer checks if the user has permission to access particular data or to perform a particular action, typically by checking if the user's roles have this permission or not.
6. **Enable Mandatory access control:** It is a security method, that restricts the ability to access resources based on the sensitivity of the information, that the resource contains. This security policy can only be controlled by the administrator, regular users don't have the ability to change that policy. Because of this centralized administration, it is considered to be very secure.

AI-enhanced techniques can play a significant role in detecting and preventing broken access control vulnerabilities, as well as in ensuring secure web and application development practices. Here's how AI can be utilized in this context:

- **Access Pattern Analysis:** AI algorithms can analyze access patterns and user behaviors to identify potential instances of broken access control. By monitoring user interactions with the application, AI systems can detect anomalies such as unauthorized access attempts or unusual access patterns that may indicate broken access control.
- **Role-Based Access Control (RBAC):** AI-powered systems can assist in implementing and managing RBAC policies within web applications. By analyzing user roles, permissions, and access patterns, AI models can help ensure that access control policies are properly configured and enforced, reducing the risk of unauthorized access.
- **Dynamic Authorization:** AI-driven dynamic authorization mechanisms can adaptively adjust access control decisions based on contextual factors such as user behavior, device characteristics, and location. By incorporating machine learning algorithms, these systems can make real-time access control decisions that account for changing threat landscapes and user contexts.
- **Predictive Access Control:** AI algorithms can predict access control policies based on historical access patterns and user attributes. By analyzing past access events and user characteristics, AI models can anticipate future access requirements and proactively enforce access control policies to prevent unauthorized access.
- **Behavioral Biometrics:** AI-based behavioral biometrics can authenticate users based on unique behavioral patterns such as typing dynamics, mouse movements, and navigation behavior. By continuously analyzing user behavior, AI systems can detect anomalies that may indicate unauthorized access attempts or account compromise.
- **Privilege Escalation Detection:** AI-driven anomaly detection techniques can identify suspicious activities that may indicate privilege escalation attempts within web applications. By analyzing user actions and access patterns, AI systems can detect unauthorized attempts to escalate privileges and trigger alerts for further investigation.
- **Audit and Compliance Monitoring:** AI-powered audit and compliance monitoring systems can ensure that access control policies are being properly enforced and that any deviations are promptly detected and remediated. By analyzing access logs and user activities, AI models can identify compliance violations and enforce corrective actions to maintain regulatory compliance.
- **Automated Policy Enforcement:** AI-driven policy enforcement mechanisms can automatically enforce access control policies based on predefined rules and machine learning models. By integrating with access control mechanisms, these systems can dynamically adjust permissions and access rights to prevent unauthorized access attempts in real-time.

By leveraging AI-enhanced techniques for access control, organizations can strengthen their defenses against broken access control vulnerabilities, reduce the risk of unauthorized access, and ensure the integrity and confidentiality of sensitive data within web and application environments.

## 4.9 SECURITY MISCONFIGURATION

Security misconfiguration occurs when security settings are not adequately defined in the configuration process or maintained and deployed with default settings. This might impact any layer of the application stack, cloud or network. Misconfigured clouds are a central cause of data breaches, costing organizations millions of dollars.

- Vulnerabilities are generally introduced during configuration. Typical misconfiguration vulnerabilities occur with the use of the following:
- Defaults—including passwords, certificates and installation
- Deprecated protocols and encryption Open database instances
- Directory listing—this should not be enabled Error messages showing sensitive information Misconfigured cloud settings
- Unnecessary features—including pages, ports and command injection

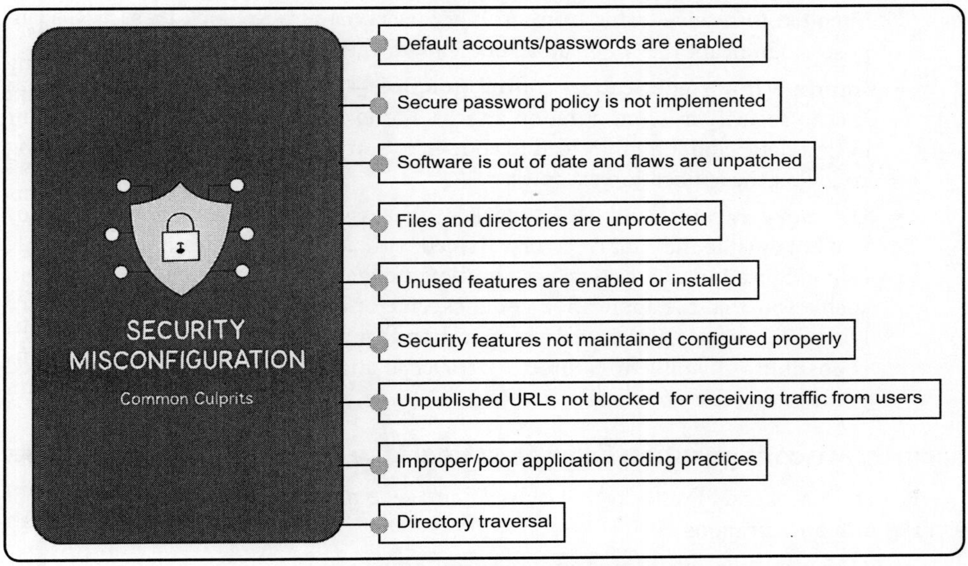


***Fig 4.11** Security MisConfiguration*

The following are common occurrences in an IT environment that can lead to a security misconfiguration:

- **Default accounts/passwords are enabled**—Using vendor-supplied defaults for system accounts and passwords is a common security misconfiguration, and may allow attackers to gain unauthorized access to the system.
- **Secure password policy is not implemented**—Failure to implement a password policy may allow attackers to gain unauthorized access to the system by methods such as using lists of common username and passwords to brute force a username and/or password field until successful authentication.
- **Software is out of date and flaws are unpatched**—Failure to update software patches as part of the software management process may allow attackers to use techniques such as code injection to inject malicious code that the application then executes.

- **Files and directories are unprotected**—Leaving files and directories unprotected may allow attackers to use techniques such as forceful browsing to gain access to restricted files or areas in the server directory.
- **Unused features are enabled or installed**—Failure to remove unnecessary features, components, documentation, and samples makes the application susceptible to misconfiguration vulnerabilities, and may allow attackers to use techniques such as code injection to inject malicious code that the application then executes.
- **Security features not maintained or configured properly**—Failure to properly configure and maintain security features makes the application vulnerable to misconfiguration attacks.
- **Unpublished URLs are not blocked from receiving traffic from ordinary users**— Unpublished URLs, accessed by those who maintain applications, are not intended to receive traffic from ordinary users. Failure to block these URLs can pose a significant risk when attackers scan for them.
- **Improper/poor application coding practices**—Improper coding practices can lead to security misconfiguration attacks. For example, the lack of proper input/output data validation may lead to code injection attacks which work by injecting code that the application executes.
- **Directory traversal**—allows an attacker to access directories, files, and commands that are outside the root directory. Armed with access to application source code or configuration and critical system files, a cybercriminal can change a URL in such a way that the application could execute or display the contents of arbitrary files on the server. Any device or application that reveals an HTTP-based interface is possibly vulnerable to a directory traversal attack. Learn more in our detailed guide to directory traversal

## Security Misconfiguration Examples: Real Like Misconfiguration Attacks

Here are a few real life attacks that caused damage to major organizations, as a result of security misconfigurations:

- **NASA authorization misconfiguration attack:** NASA because vulnerable to a misconfiguration in Atlassian JIRA. An authorization misconfiguration in Global Permissions enabled exposure of sensitive data to attackers.
- **Amazon S3:** Many organizations experienced data breaches as a result of unsecured storage buckets on Amazon's popular S3 storage service. For example, the US Army Intelligence and Security Command inadvertently stored sensitive database files, some of them marked top secret, in S3 without proper authentication.
- **Citrix legacy protocols attack:** Citrix used an IMAP-based cloud email server and became the target of IMAP-based password-spraying. IMAP is an insecure, legacy protocol, and attackers exploited it to get access to cloud-based accounts and SaaS applications. Using multi factor authentication (MFA) could have stopped the attack.
- **Mirai botnet:** Mirai was a mega-scale botnet that infected network devices like CCTV cameras, DVD devices and home routers. The botnet exploited a misconfiguration in these devices – the use of insecure default passwords. The botnet was used to carry out DDoS attacks of unprecedented magnitude, which brought down websites like Twitter, Reddit, and Netflix.

Security misconfigurations are common yet critical vulnerabilities that can lead to significant risks in web and application security. These misconfigurations can arise from improper setup or maintenance of security controls, leaving systems vulnerable to exploitation. AI-enhanced techniques can play a crucial role in both identifying and preventing security misconfigurations, as well as improving the overall security posture of web and application environments. Here's how AI can be utilized:

- **Configuration Analysis:** AI-driven tools can automatically analyze system configurations to identify potential misconfigurations. By comparing configurations against security best practices and known vulnerabilities, these tools can flag insecure settings that may lead to security breaches.
- **Automated Remediation:** AI systems can provide automated recommendations for remediation of security misconfigurations. By analyzing the impact of configuration changes and potential security implications, these systems can suggest corrective actions to mitigate risks effectively.
- **Continuous Monitoring:** AI-driven monitoring solutions can continuously monitor system configurations for changes and deviations from secure baselines. By leveraging machine learning algorithms, these solutions can detect anomalous configuration changes that may indicate unauthorized access or tampering.
- **Vulnerability Assessment:** AI-powered vulnerability assessment tools can identify security misconfigurations as part of the broader vulnerability scanning process. By analyzing system configurations alongside other security controls, these tools can provide a comprehensive view of security posture and prioritize remediation efforts.
- **Policy Enforcement:** AI-enhanced systems can enforce security policies and standards by automatically verifying compliance with predefined configuration guidelines. By analyzing configurations in real-time and comparing them against security policies, these systems can ensure that systems adhere to security best practices.
- Risk Assessment: AI-driven risk assessment frameworks can quantify the potential impact of security misconfigurations on overall risk posture. By considering factors such as the criticality of misconfigurations and their likelihood of exploitation, these frameworks can prioritize mitigation efforts based on risk severity.
- **User Behavior Analytics:** AI-based user behavior analytics can detect anomalous administrative activities that may indicate unauthorized configuration changes. By analyzing patterns of administrative behavior and comparing them against historical data, these systems can identify suspicious activities that require investigation.
- **Training and Education:** AI-powered training platforms can educate developers and administrators about secure configuration practices. By leveraging machine learning techniques to personalize training materials and simulate real-world scenarios, these platforms can improve awareness and knowledge of security best practices.

By integrating AI-enhanced techniques into configuration management processes and security controls, organizations can effectively identify and mitigate security misconfigurations, reducing the risk of data breaches and unauthorized access in web and application environments.

## 4.10 CROSS-SITE SCRIPTING (XSS)

Cross Site Scripting (XSS) is a vulnerability in a web application that allows a third party to execute a script in the user's browser on behalf of the web application. Cross-site Scripting is one of the most prevalent vulnerabilities present on the web today. The exploitation of XSS against a user can lead to various consequences such as account compromise, account deletion, privilege escalation, malware infection and many more.

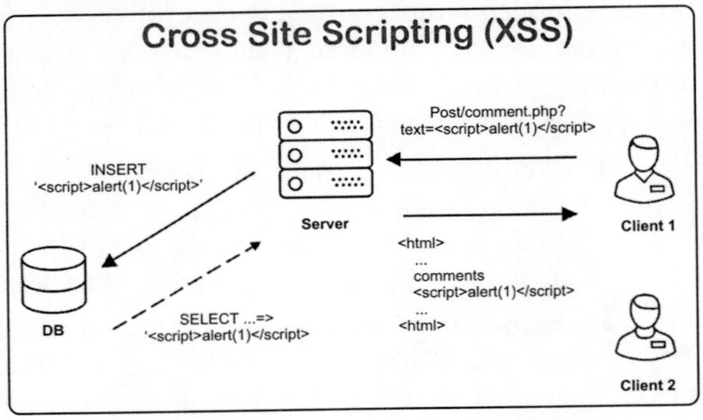


*Fig 4.12 Cross Site Scripting (XSS)*

- **Reflected XSS:** If the input has to be provided each time to execute, such XSS is called reflected. These attacks are mostly carried out by delivering a payload directly to the victim. Victim requests a page with a request containing the payload and the payload comes embedded in the response as a script. An example of reflected XSS is XSS in the search field.

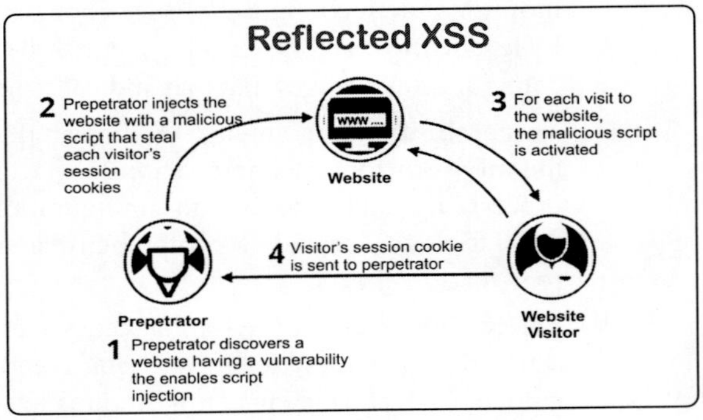


*Fig : 4.13 Reflected XSS*

- **Stored XSS:** When the response containing the payload is stored on the server in such a way that the script gets executed on every visit without submission of payload, then it is identified as stored XSS. An example of stored XSS is XSS in the comment thread.

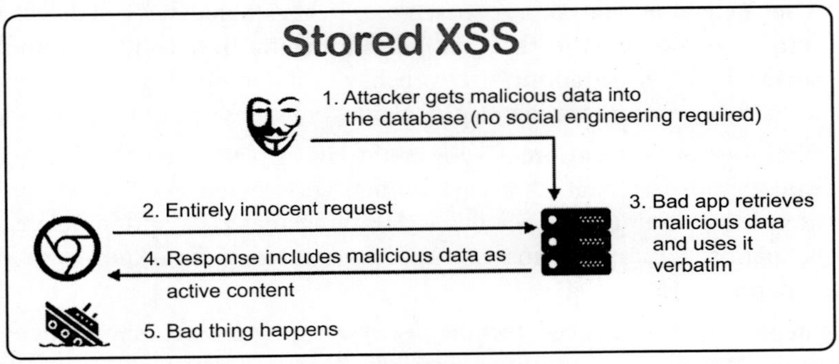


*Fig 4.14 Stored XSS*

Security misconfigurations are common yet critical vulnerabilities that can lead to significant risks in web and application security. These misconfigurations can arise from improper setup or maintenance of security controls, leaving systems vulnerable to exploitation. AI-enhanced techniques can play a crucial role in both identifying and preventing security misconfigurations, as well as improving the overall security posture of web and application environments. Here's how AI can be utilized:

- **Configuration Analysis:** AI-driven tools can automatically analyze system configurations to identify potential misconfigurations. By comparing configurations against security best practices and known vulnerabilities, these tools can flag insecure settings that may lead to security breaches.
- **Automated Remediation:** AI systems can provide automated recommendations for remediation of security misconfigurations. By analyzing the impact of configuration changes and potential security implications, these systems can suggest corrective actions to mitigate risks effectively.
- **Continuous Monitoring:** AI-driven monitoring solutions can continuously monitor system configurations for changes and deviations from secure baselines. By leveraging machine learning algorithms, these solutions can detect anomalous configuration changes that may indicate unauthorized access or tampering.
- **Vulnerability Assessment:** AI-powered vulnerability assessment tools can identify security misconfigurations as part of the broader vulnerability scanning process. By analyzing system configurations alongside other security controls, these tools can provide a comprehensive view of security posture and prioritize remediation efforts.
- **Policy Enforcement:** AI-enhanced systems can enforce security policies and standards by automatically verifying compliance with predefined configuration guidelines. By analyzing configurations in real-time and comparing them against security policies, these systems can ensure that systems adhere to security best practices.
- **Risk Assessment:** AI-driven risk assessment frameworks can quantify the potential impact of security misconfigurations on overall risk posture. By considering factors such as the criticality of misconfigurations and their likelihood of exploitation, these frameworks can prioritize mitigation efforts based on risk severity.
- **User Behavior Analytics:** AI-based user behavior analytics can detect anomalous administrative activities that may indicate unauthorized configuration changes. By analyzing patterns of administrative behavior and comparing them against historical data, these systems can identify suspicious activities that require investigation.
- **Training and Education:** AI-powered training platforms can educate developers and administrators about secure configuration practices. By leveraging machine learning techniques to personalize training materials and simulate real-world scenarios, these platforms can improve awareness and knowledge of security best practices.

By integrating AI-enhanced techniques into configuration management processes and security controls, organizations can effectively identify and mitigate security misconfigurations, reducing the risk of data breaches and unauthorized access in web and application environments. Serialization is the process of transforming a binary complex object into a simple format that can be transferred and easily manipulated. On the other hand, Deserialization is the opposite action, where this simple format is interpreted by the programing language to forge an actual binary object.

By serializing an object, this one can be saved in a file system to be used again with the same or different program or even sent to another computer with a network connection. What makes this concept even more important is the fact that the serialized objects are platform- independent. Therefore, an object created and manipulated in host 1 will still be the same when transferred to host 2 even if they don't use the same architecture.

## 4.11 INSECURE DESERIALIZATION

Vulnerability that occurs when untrusted data is deserialized by an application without proper validation, leading to potential remote code execution, denial of service, or other security risks. AI-enhanced techniques can be valuable in both detecting and preventing insecure deserialization vulnerabilities, as well as improving the overall security of web and application development practices.

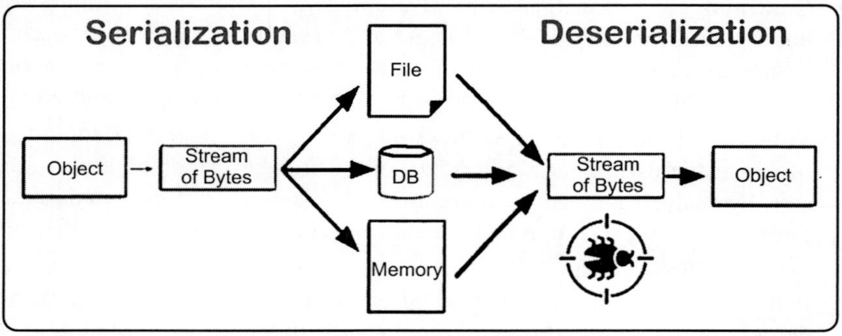


***Fig 4.15*** *Insecure deserialization*

- **Pattern Recognition:** AI algorithms can be trained to recognize patterns indicative of insecure deserialization vulnerabilities in application code. By analyzing deserialization routines and data handling practices, AI models can identify insecure deserialization points that may lead to security breaches.
- **Static Code Analysis:** AI-powered static code analysis tools can automatically scan source code for insecure deserialization vulnerabilities. By analyzing deserialization logic and data flow, these tools can identify potential points of exploitation and insecure deserialization practices that may lead to security vulnerabilities.
- **Dynamic Code Analysis:** AI-driven dynamic code analysis tools can execute applications in a controlled environment to detect runtime insecure deserialization vulnerabilities. By monitoring data flows and analyzing deserialization behaviors, these tools can identify instances where untrusted data is improperly processed, leading to security risks.
- **Input Validation:** AI-driven input validation mechanisms can help detect and prevent insecure deserialization attacks by analyzing serialized data for potentially malicious content. By learning from past attacks and known insecure deserialization patterns, AI systems can identify and filter out dangerous serialized objects that could trigger vulnerabilities.
- **Behavioral Analysis:** AI-based behavioral analysis techniques can monitor application behavior to detect abnormal deserialization activities that may indicate insecure deserialization attacks. By learning the normal behavior of

deserialization routines, AI systems can identify deviations caused by insecure deserialization vulnerabilities and trigger alerts or block malicious requests.

- **Patch Management:** AI systems can assist in prioritizing patch management efforts by analyzing the potential impact of insecure deserialization vulnerabilities on application security. By considering factors such as exploitability and business criticality, AI models can help organizations prioritize and apply patches to mitigate risks effectively.
- **User Behavior Analytics:** AI-driven user behavior analytics can detect anomalies in user interactions with deserialization functionalities, which may indicate insecure deserialization attacks. By analyzing patterns of deserialization usage, data input, and processing behavior, these systems can identify suspicious activities that warrant further investigation.

By integrating AI-enhanced techniques into the development lifecycle and runtime monitoring of web and application environments, organizations can strengthen their defenses against insecure deserialization vulnerabilities, mitigate risks, and enhance overall security posture.

## 4.12 USING COMPONENTS WITH KNOWN VULNERABILITIES AND INSUFFICIENT LOGGING AND MONITORING

### Using Components With Known Vulnerabilities

Components such as libraries, frameworks are themselves vulnerable. They could be dangerous for application as it enables various attacks and impacts. If a vulnerable component gets exploited, then an attack can lead to serious data loss or server takeover.

Best practices to be followed:

- Do not keep any unused dependencies, libraries, files, and components.
- Track client-side, server-side component versions for security vulnerabilities and patches.
- Get components, libraries only from trusted and official sources.

### Insufficient Logging And Monitoring

This may allow attackers to further attack the systems, tamper, extract or destroy the data. This insufficient logging will lead to problems like breaches getting informed by external parties instead of getting detected from internal monitoring.

Best practices to be followed:

- Ensure all types of loggings for failures, validations, user contexts, integrity checks which can find out any malicious activity if any.
- Ensure all logs have a certain format that can be easily consumed by log management solutions.
- Establish effective monitoring and alerting for suspicious activities.

Addressing vulnerabilities related to using components with known vulnerabilities and insufficient logging and monitoring is crucial for ensuring the security of web and application environments. AI-enhanced techniques can be beneficial in both identifying and mitigating these vulnerabilities, as well as enhancing overall security practices. Here's how AI can be utilized:

- **Vulnerability Management:** AI-powered vulnerability management solutions can automatically scan applications and dependencies to identify components with known vulnerabilities. By leveraging machine learning algorithms to prioritize vulnerabilities based on severity and exploitability, these solutions can assist in patch management efforts and reducing the risk of exploitation.
- **Patch Prioritization:** AI systems can assist in prioritizing patch management efforts by analyzing the potential impact of known vulnerabilities on application security. By considering factors such as exploitability, attack surface, and business criticality, AI models can help organizations prioritize and apply patches effectively to mitigate risks.
- **Dependency Analysis:** AI-driven dependency analysis tools can identify and track dependencies within applications, including third-party libraries and frameworks. By monitoring for updates and security advisories related to these dependencies, AI systems can help ensure that applications are using the latest versions with known vulnerabilities patched.
- **Automated Remediation:** AI-powered remediation tools can provide automated recommendations for addressing vulnerabilities related to known components. By analyzing the impact of potential fixes and suggesting appropriate mitigation strategies, these tools can streamline the remediation process and reduce the window of exposure to vulnerabilities.
- **Behavioral Analysis:** AI-based behavioral analysis techniques can monitor application behavior to detect suspicious activities that may indicate exploitation of known vulnerabilities. By learning the normal behavior of applications and users, AI systems can identify deviations that may signal security incidents and trigger alerts for further investigation.
- **Log Analysis:** AI-driven log analysis solutions can help identify security incidents and anomalies in application logs. By analyzing log data for patterns indicative of malicious activity, AI systems can assist in detecting and responding to attacks exploiting known vulnerabilities.
- **Real-time Monitoring:** AI-enhanced monitoring solutions can provide real-time visibility into application activity and security events. By correlating data from various sources, including logs, network traffic, and user behavior, AI systems can help detect and respond to attacks targeting known vulnerabilities promptly.
- **Threat Intelligence Integration:** AI systems can integrate with threat intelligence feeds to provide context and prioritize security alerts related to known vulnerabilities. By analyzing threat intelligence data and mapping it to known vulnerabilities, AI models can help organizations stay informed about emerging threats and potential exploitation of known weaknesses.

By incorporating AI-enhanced techniques into vulnerability management, patch prioritization, dependency analysis, logging and monitoring, organizations can enhance their ability to detect, mitigate, and respond to threats associated with using components with known vulnerabilities and insufficient logging and monitoring in web and application environments.

◆◆◆

# UNIT 5

# Cyber Threats

## 5.1 FUTURE OF AI IN ADVANCING SECURITY AND PROMOTING, ARTIFICIAL INTELLIGENCE VS. DATA ANALYTICS

The future of AI in advancing security and promoting safety is promising, as AI technologies continue to evolve and integrate into various aspects of security systems. Here are some key points regarding the future of AI in security:

- **Advanced Threat Detection:** AI-powered algorithms can analyze large volumes of data to detect patterns and anomalies that may indicate potential security threats. These algorithms can continuously learn and adapt to new threats, making them more effective than traditional methods.
- **Behavioral Analysis:** AI can be used to analyze user behavior and detect suspicious activities in real-time. This includes monitoring network traffic, user activity, and system logs to identify abnormal behavior that may indicate a security breach.
- **Automation of Security Processes:** AI can automate routine security tasks such as monitoring, incident response, and vulnerability assessments. This frees up human resources to focus on more strategic tasks and enables faster response times to security incidents.
- **Predictive Analytics:** AI can leverage predictive analytics to anticipate security threats before they occur. By analyzing historical data and identifying patterns, AI systems can proactively identify potential vulnerabilities and weaknesses in security systems.
- **Enhanced Authentication Methods:** AI can improve authentication methods by implementing biometric authentication, facial recognition, voice recognition, and other advanced techniques to verify user identities more securely.
- **Securing IoT Devices:** With the proliferation of Internet of Things (IoT) devices, AI can play a crucial role in securing these devices and networks. AI algorithms can monitor IoT devices for suspicious behavior and mitigate security risks in real-time.
- **Privacy Concerns:** As AI systems become more prevalent in security applications, there are growing concerns about privacy and data protection. It's essential to implement robust privacy measures and adhere to regulations such as GDPR to ensure that personal data is adequately protected.

## 5.2 ARTIFICIAL INTELLIGENCE (AI) AND DATA ANALYTICS

- **Artificial Intelligence (AI):** AI refers to the simulation of human intelligence in machines that are programmed to think and learn like humans. AI encompasses various technologies such as machine learning, natural language processing, computer vision, and deep learning. In the context of security, AI can be used to detect threats, automate security processes, and enhance decision-making capabilities.
- **Data Analytics:** Data analytics involves analyzing raw data to extract meaningful insights and make informed decisions. It encompasses various techniques such as descriptive analytics, diagnostic analytics, predictive analytics, and prescriptive analytics. In the context of security, data analytics can be used to identify trends, patterns, and anomalies in data that may indicate security threats or vulnerabilities.

While AI and data analytics are closely related and often used together, there are some key differences between the two:

- **Focus:** AI focuses on simulating human intelligence and learning from data to make decisions autonomously, while data analytics focuses on extracting insights from data to inform decision- making.
- **Techniques:** AI encompasses a broader range of techniques, including machine learning, natural language processing, and computer vision, while data analytics primarily involves statistical and mathematical techniques for analyzing data.
- **Automation:** AI often involves automating tasks and decision-making processes based on learned patterns and algorithms, while data analytics may involve manual analysis and interpretation of data by human analysts.

In summary, while AI and data analytics are distinct concepts, they are closely related and can complement each other in advancing security and promoting safety through the analysis of data and the implementation of intelligent algorithms and systems.

## 5.3 APPLYING AI TO CYBERSECURITY, SOME EARLY AI ADOPTERS

AI Use by Adversaries Applying AI to cybersecurity offers numerous benefits, including enhanced threat detection, faster incident response, and improved overall security posture. Some early adopters of AI in cybersecurity include:

- **Endpoint Security:** AI-powered endpoint security solutions can detect and respond to threats in real-time, protecting devices such as laptops, desktops, and mobile devices from malware, ransomware, and other cyber threats.
- **Network Security:** AI-based network security solutions can analyze network traffic patterns to detect anomalies and potential security breaches. These solutions can identify suspicious activities such as unauthorized access attempts, data exfiltration, and insider threats.
- **Threat Intelligence:** AI can analyze vast amounts of threat intelligence data to identify emerging threats and vulnerabilities. By correlating threat data from multiple sources, AI- powered threat intelligence platforms can provide organizations with actionable insights to proactively defend against cyber attacks.

- **User Behavior Analytics:** AI can analyze user behavior to detect unusual patterns that may indicate insider threats or compromised accounts. By monitoring user activity across systems and applications, AI-powered user behavior analytics solutions can identify potential security risks and mitigate them before they escalate.
- **Security Orchestration and Automation:** AI-driven security orchestration and automation platforms can streamline security operations by automating routine tasks such as incident triage, investigation, and response. These platforms can help security teams improve efficiency and effectiveness in responding to security incidents.

While AI offers significant benefits for cybersecurity, adversaries are also leveraging AI technologies to enhance their attack capabilities. Some ways in which adversaries are using AI include:

- **Automated Attacks:** Adversaries can use AI-powered tools to automate various stages of the cyber attack lifecycle, including reconnaissance, exploitation, and exfiltration. These automated attacks can be more efficient and effective than traditional manual attacks.

## 5.4 AI USE BY ADVERSARIES

Adversaries can exploit vulnerabilities in AI-based security systems by poisoning training data, manipulating algorithms, or evading detection using adversarial machine learning techniques. This can undermine the effectiveness of AI-powered security defenses.

- **Social Engineering:** AI can be used to generate highly convincing phishing emails, voice calls, or chatbots that impersonate legitimate individuals or organizations. These AI-powered social engineering attacks can trick users into divulging sensitive information or downloading malware.
- **Evasion Techniques:** Adversaries can use AI to develop evasion techniques that bypass traditional security controls such as antivirus software, intrusion detection systems, and firewalls. By dynamically adjusting their attack strategies based on AI-driven detection mechanisms, adversaries can evade detection and prolong their presence within target networks.

Overall, while AI holds great promise for improving cybersecurity defenses, it also presents new challenges and risks that organizations must address to stay ahead of evolving cyber threats. Vigilance, robust security measures, and ongoing innovation will be essential for effectively harnessing the power of AI in cybersecurity while mitigating its potential risks.

## 5.5 USING ARTIFICIAL INTELLIGENCE TOOLS TO ENHANCE SECURITY

Artificial intelligence (AI) tools offer a wide range of capabilities to enhance security across various domains. Here are some ways in which AI tools can be used to strengthen security:

- **Threat Detection and Prevention:** AI-powered threat detection systems can analyze large volumes of data in real-time to identify patterns and anomalies indicative of security threats. These systems can detect various types of threats, including malware, ransomware, phishing attacks, and insider threats, enabling organizations to take proactive measures to prevent security breaches.

- **Anomaly Detection:** AI-based anomaly detection systems can monitor user and system behavior to identify deviations from normal patterns. By detecting suspicious activities or behaviors that may indicate a security breach, these systems can help organizations quickly respond to potential threats and minimize the impact of security incidents.
- **Predictive Analytics:** AI can leverage predictive analytics to anticipate security threats before they occur. By analyzing historical data and identifying patterns, AI systems can forecast potential security risks and vulnerabilities, allowing organizations to implement preventive measures and mitigate risks proactively.
- **User Authentication and Access Control:** AI-powered authentication systems can enhance security by implementing advanced authentication methods such as biometric recognition, facial recognition, and behavioral biometrics. These systems can verify user identities more securely and prevent unauthorized access to sensitive data and resources.
- **Security Orchestration and Automation:** AI-driven security orchestration and automation platforms can streamline security operations by automating routine tasks such as incident response, threat analysis, and remediation. By automating manual processes and workflows, these platforms can improve efficiency, reduce response times, and enable security teams to focus on more strategic tasks.
- **Natural Language Processing (NLP):** NLP-powered systems can analyze unstructured data sources such as text-based communications, social media, and online forums to identify potential security threats and vulnerabilities. By extracting insights from unstructured data, NLP systems can provide valuable intelligence to help organizations better understand and mitigate security risks.
- **Vulnerability Management:** AI can enhance vulnerability management processes by automatically identifying and prioritizing security vulnerabilities based on their severity, exploitability, and potential impact on the organization. AI-powered vulnerability management systems can help organizations efficiently allocate resources to address the most critical vulnerabilities and reduce their exposure to cyber threats.

Overall, AI tools offer significant potential to enhance security by improving threat detection and prevention, enabling more effective incident response, and enhancing overall security posture. By leveraging the capabilities of AI, organizations can better protect their systems, data, and assets from evolving cyber threats.

## 5.6 DEEP LEARNING APPLICATIONS

Deep learning, a subset of artificial intelligence, has found significant applications in enhancing cyber threats for malicious purposes. Here are several ways in which deep learning is used to amplify cyber threats:

- **Advanced Malware Creation:** Deep learning algorithms can be utilized to generate sophisticated malware that is more evasive and difficult to detect by traditional security solutions. These algorithms can learn from vast amounts of data to develop new malware variants that can bypass antivirus software and other security defenses.
- **Targeted Phishing Attacks:** Deep learning techniques can be employed to create

highly convincing phishing emails that are tailored to specific individuals or organizations. By analyzing data from social media profiles, emails, and other sources, deep learning algorithms can generate personalized phishing messages that are more likely to deceive recipients into disclosing sensitive information or clicking on malicious links.

- **Adversarial Attacks:** Deep learning models are susceptible to adversarial attacks, where subtle modifications are made to input data to deceive the model into making incorrect predictions. Adversaries can exploit vulnerabilities in deep learning algorithms to manipulate security systems, such as bypassing image-based authentication systems or fooling malware detection systems.
- **Fake News and Disinformation:** Deep learning can be used to generate fake news articles, videos, and audio recordings that are indistinguishable from genuine content. These synthetic media can be used to spread disinformation, manipulate public opinion, and undermine trust in institutions, leading to social unrest and political instability.
- **Automated Exploitation:** Deep learning algorithms can automate the process of identifying and exploiting security vulnerabilities in software and networks. By analyzing code and network traffic data, these algorithms can identify exploitable weaknesses that can be leveraged to gain unauthorized access to systems or steal sensitive information.
- **IoT Botnets:** Deep learning can be used to create intelligent botnets that can infect and control Internet of Things (IoT) devices. These botnets can launch large-scale distributed denial-of- service (DDoS) attacks, spread malware, and perform other malicious activities, posing significant threats to network infrastructure and critical services.
- **Deepfake Attacks:** Deep learning techniques can be employed to create convincing deepfake videos and audio recordings that impersonate individuals or manipulate their words and actions. These deepfake attacks can be used for blackmail, extortion, or discrediting individuals and organizations.

Overall, deep learning has the potential to significantly amplify cyber threats by enabling the creation of more sophisticated malware, targeted phishing attacks, adversarial attacks, fake news and disinformation campaigns, automated exploitation of vulnerabilities, IoT botnets, and deepfake attacks. As deep learning continues to advance, it is essential for organizations to develop robust cybersecurity strategies and defenses to mitigate these emerging threats effectively.

## 5.7 CYBER SECURITY THREATS AND DEVELOPMENT OF SECURE SOFTWARE

Cybersecurity threats are continuously evolving, posing significant challenges to organizations worldwide. Developing secure software is crucial for mitigating these threats and protecting sensitive data and systems. Here are some common cybersecurity threats and strategies for developing secure software:

- **Malware:** Malware, including viruses, worms, ransomware, and spyware, poses a significant threat to software systems. To mitigate this threat, developers should implement secure coding practices, such as input validation, output encoding, and proper error handling, to prevent vulnerabilities that could be exploited by malware.

- **Phishing Attacks:** Phishing attacks involve tricking users into revealing sensitive information or installing malware through deceptive emails, websites, or messages. Secure software development practices should include implementing email authentication mechanisms, such as SPF, DKIM, and DMARC, to prevent email spoofing and phishing attacks. Additionally, developers should educate users about phishing techniques and encourage them to verify the authenticity of communications before clicking on links or providing sensitive information.
- **SQL Injection:** SQL injection attacks occur when malicious actors exploit vulnerabilities in web applications to execute arbitrary SQL commands and gain unauthorized access to databases. To prevent SQL injection attacks, developers should use parameterized queries and prepared statements, input validation, and output encoding to sanitize user input and prevent SQL injection vulnerabilities in software applications.
- **Cross-Site Scripting (XSS):** XSS attacks involve injecting malicious scripts into web pages viewed by other users. Developers should implement security controls, such as input validation, output encoding, and content security policies, to prevent XSS vulnerabilities in web applications. Additionally, developers should regularly audit and sanitize user-generated content to mitigate the risk of XSS attacks.
- **Zero-Day Exploits:** Zero-day exploits target previously unknown vulnerabilities in software applications, making them challenging to detect and mitigate. To reduce the risk of zero-day exploits, developers should follow secure coding practices, perform regular security assessments and code reviews, and promptly apply security patches and updates to software applications to address known vulnerabilities.
- **Insider Threats:** Insider threats involve malicious or negligent actions by individuals within an organization, such as employees, contractors, or partners, to compromise sensitive data or systems. Developers should implement access controls, user authentication mechanisms, and auditing/logging mechanisms to monitor and prevent unauthorized access to sensitive data and systems. Additionally, developers should enforce the principle of least privilege to limit users' access to only the resources and functionality required to perform their job duties.
- **Supply Chain Attacks:** Supply chain attacks target vulnerabilities in third-party software components, libraries, or dependencies used by software applications. Developers should carefully vet and validate third-party components, regularly update dependencies to address known vulnerabilities, and implement secure coding practices to prevent supply chain attacks.

In summary, developing secure software requires implementing secure coding practices, conducting regular security assessments and code reviews, educating developers and users about cybersecurity best practices, and promptly addressing known vulnerabilities and security threats. By adopting a proactive approach to cybersecurity and integrating security into the software development lifecycle, organizations can mitigate cybersecurity threats and protect sensitive data and systems from exploitation by malicious actors.

## 5.8 SECURING IOT INFRASTRUCTURE

Securing IoT (Internet of Things) infrastructure is becoming increasingly critical as the number of connected devices continues to grow. While AI (Artificial Intelligence) can offer valuable capabilities in enhancing IoT security, it also presents new challenges as cyber threats evolve. Here's how AI can be both a solution and a threat in securing IoT infrastructure:

### AI for Securing IoT Infrastructure

- **Anomaly Detection:** AI algorithms can analyze IoT device behavior and network traffic patterns to detect anomalies indicative of potential security breaches or abnormal device behavior.
- **Behavioral Analysis:** AI-powered systems can learn normal behavior patterns of IoT devices and users to identify deviations that may signal security threats, such as unauthorized access or malicious activity.
- **Threat Intelligence:** AI can analyze vast amounts of threat intelligence data to identify emerging threats and vulnerabilities relevant to IoT devices, allowing organizations to proactively defend against cyber attacks.
- **Device Authentication:** AI can enhance device authentication mechanisms by implementing biometric recognition, behavioral biometrics, or other advanced authentication techniques to verify the identity of IoT devices and prevent unauthorized access.
- **Network Security:** AI-driven network security solutions can monitor IoT device communications, detect suspicious activities, and enforce access controls to protect against unauthorized access and data breaches.

### AI-Enhanced Cyber Threats to IoT Infrastructure

- **Adversarial Attacks:** Adversaries can exploit vulnerabilities in AI-based security systems by poisoning training data, manipulating algorithms, or crafting adversarial examples to evade detection and compromise IoT devices.
- **Sophisticated Malware:** AI can be used to create more sophisticated malware that targets IoT devices, such as ransomware, botnets, or advanced persistent threats (APTs), making them more challenging to detect and mitigate.
- **Evasion Techniques:** Adversaries can leverage AI to develop evasion techniques that bypass traditional security controls, such as intrusion detection systems (IDS) or firewalls, allowing them to infiltrate IoT networks and carry out malicious activities undetected.
- **Deepfake Attacks:** Deep learning techniques can be used to create convincing deepfake videos or audio recordings that impersonate legitimate IoT device commands or communications, leading to unauthorized access or manipulation of IoT devices.
- **Data Poisoning:** Adversaries can manipulate data collected by IoT devices to poison AI models used for security analytics, leading to false positives or negatives in threat detection and response.

### Strategies to Mitigate AI-Enhanced Cyber Threats to IoT Infrastructure

- **Adversarial Training:** Implementing adversarial training techniques to make AI models more robust against adversarial attacks and ensure their effectiveness in detecting and mitigating threats.
- **Model Interpretability:** Enhancing the interpretability of AI models to better understand their decision-making process and identify potential vulnerabilities or biases that could be exploited by adversaries.
- **Security by Design:** Integrating security into the design and development of IoT devices and AI systems from the outset to minimize vulnerabilities and mitigate potential risks to IoT infrastructure.
- **Continuous Monitoring and Updating:** Regularly monitoring IoT devices and AI systems for security vulnerabilities, updating firmware and software patches, and applying security updates to address emerging threats.
- **Multi-Layered Defense:** Implementing a multi-layered security approach that combines AI- powered threat detection and prevention with traditional security controls, such as encryption, access controls, and network segmentation, to protect IoT infrastructure from cyber threats effectively.

In conclusion, while AI offers valuable capabilities in enhancing IoT security, it also introduces new challenges and risks that organizations must address to safeguard IoT infrastructure against cyber threats effectively. By implementing proactive security measures and adopting a holistic approach to cybersecurity, organizations can mitigate the risks posed by AI-enhanced cyber threats and protect their IoT infrastructure from malicious actors.

## 5.9 SECURE AI DEVELOPMENT

Secure AI development is essential to mitigate the risks posed by AI-enhanced cyber threats. Here are some considerations and best practices for developing AI systems securely, along with potential cyber threats enhanced by AI:

### Secure AI Development Best Practices

- **Data Privacy and Security:** Implement robust data privacy and security measures to protect sensitive data used for training AI models, such as encryption, access controls, and anonymization techniques.
- **Model Robustness Testing:** Perform rigorous testing and validation of AI models to identify vulnerabilities, biases, and adversarial examples that could be exploited by attackers.
- **Secure Coding Practices:** Follow secure coding practices when developing AI algorithms and applications to prevent common vulnerabilities, such as input validation errors, buffer overflows, and injection attacks.
- **Authentication and Access Control:** Implement strong authentication mechanisms and access controls to protect AI systems from unauthorized access and manipulation by attackers.
- **Model Explainability and Transparency:** Enhance the explainability and transparency of AI models to understand their decision-making process and identify potential security risks or biases.

- **Secure Deployment and Configuration:** Securely deploy and configure AI systems in production environments, following best practices for network security, system hardening, and software patch management.
- **Continuous Monitoring and Incident Response:** Continuously monitor AI systems for security threats and anomalies, and establish incident response procedures to mitigate security incidents promptly.

## AI-Enhanced Cyber Threats

- **Adversarial Attacks:** Adversarial attacks exploit vulnerabilities in AI models by injecting malicious inputs or perturbations to manipulate their output, leading to incorrect decisions or predictions.
- **Data Poisoning:** Attackers can manipulate training data used to train AI models to introduce biases or malicious patterns, compromising the integrity and accuracy of the models.
- **Privacy Breaches:** AI systems may inadvertently disclose sensitive or personally identifiable information during the training or inference process, leading to privacy breaches and regulatory non-compliance.
- **Model Theft and Reverse Engineering:** Attackers may attempt to steal proprietary AI models or reverse-engineer them to understand their underlying algorithms and replicate their functionality for malicious purposes.
- **Model Evasion and Manipulation:** Attackers can attempt to evade detection by AI-based security systems or manipulate their input to bypass security controls and exploit vulnerabilities in target systems.
- **Poisoning Federated Learning:** Federated learning, which involves training AI models on decentralized data sources, may be susceptible to poisoning attacks where malicious participants inject corrupted data to compromise the integrity of the trained models.
- **Deepfake Attacks:** Deep learning techniques can be used to create convincing deepfake videos or audio recordings that impersonate individuals or manipulate their words and actions, leading to social engineering attacks or disinformation campaigns.

## Mitigating AI-Enhanced Cyber Threats

- **Adversarial Training:** Train AI models with adversarial examples to make them more robust against adversarial attacks and improve their resilience to manipulation.
- **Model Validation and Testing:** Conduct thorough validation and testing of AI models to identify vulnerabilities and biases, and employ techniques such as differential privacy to protect sensitive data.
- **Data Governance and Protection:** Implement data governance policies and data protection mechanisms to ensure the integrity, confidentiality, and privacy of training data used for AI models.
- **Model Explainability and Transparency:** Enhance the explainability and transparency of AI models to understand their decision-making process and detect anomalous or suspicious behavior.

- **Continuous Monitoring and Response:** Continuously monitor AI systems for security threats and anomalies, and establish incident response procedures to mitigate security incidents promptly.

By following these best practices and mitigating AI-enhanced cyber threats, organizations can develop and deploy AI systems securely while protecting sensitive data and systems from exploitation by malicious actors.

## 5.10 LARGE SCALE DEPLOYMENT OF AI ALGORITHMS ON PRODUCTION

Large-scale deployment of AI algorithms in production environments introduces unique cybersecurity challenges. While AI can enhance security measures, it can also be exploited by cyber threats. Here are some AI-enhanced cyber threats to consider when deploying AI algorithms at scale:

- **Adversarial Attacks:** Attackers can manipulate input data to AI algorithms to produce incorrect outputs, causing the algorithms to make wrong decisions. Adversarial attacks can lead to security breaches or system malfunctions, especially in critical applications such as autonomous vehicles or healthcare systems.
- **Model Poisoning:** Malicious actors may inject poisoned data into the training datasets used for AI algorithms, compromising the integrity and reliability of the models. Model poisoning can lead to biased or inaccurate predictions, affecting the performance of AI systems in production environments.
- **Privacy Violations:** AI algorithms may inadvertently expose sensitive or personally identifiable information during data processing or inference. Privacy violations can occur if AI systems are not properly designed to protect confidential data, leading to regulatory non- compliance and reputational damage.
- **Data Breaches:** AI systems rely on vast amounts of data, which increases the risk of data breaches if the data is not adequately protected. Attackers may target AI algorithms to gain unauthorized access to sensitive data, leading to data theft or leakage.
- **Model Theft and Reverse Engineering:** Intellectual property theft is a significant concern in AI deployments, as attackers may attempt to steal proprietary AI models or reverse-engineer them to replicate their functionality. Stolen models can be used to create counterfeit products or services, undermining the competitive advantage of organizations.
- **Evasion and Manipulation:** Attackers can exploit vulnerabilities in AI algorithms to evade detection by security systems or manipulate their output for malicious purposes. Evasion and manipulation techniques can be used to bypass security controls, infiltrate networks, or launch cyber attacks without detection.
- **Deepfake Attacks:** Deep learning techniques can be used to create convincing deepfake videos or audio recordings that impersonate individuals or manipulate their words and actions. Deepfake attacks can be used for social engineering, disinformation campaigns, or blackmail, posing significant risks to organizations and individuals.

Mitigating AI-enhanced cyber threats in large-scale deployments requires a multi-faceted approach:

- **Robust Security Measures:** Implement robust security measures to protect AI algorithms, data, and infrastructure from cyber threats, including encryption, access controls, and network segmentation.
- **Continuous Monitoring and Detection:** Monitor AI systems for suspicious activities or anomalies and deploy advanced detection techniques, such as anomaly detection or behavioral analysis, to identify potential security breaches.
- **Adversarial Training:** Train AI algorithms with adversarial examples to improve their resilience to adversarial attacks and enhance their security posture in production environments.
- **Data Governance and Privacy Protection:** Implement data governance policies and privacy protection mechanisms to ensure the confidentiality, integrity, and privacy of sensitive data used by AI systems.
- **Model Explainability and Transparency:** Enhance the explainability and transparency of AI algorithms to understand their decision-making process and detect potential vulnerabilities or biases.
- **Regular Updates and Patch Management:** Keep AI algorithms and infrastructure up to date with the latest security patches and updates to address known vulnerabilities and protect against emerging threats.

By addressing these challenges and implementing appropriate security measures, organizations can deploy AI algorithms at scale while mitigating the risks posed by AI-enhanced cyber threats.

## CASE STUDY: SECURE IOT APPLICATION IN A DEVELOPED ECOSYSTEM

### 1. Design and Planning Phase

- **Scenario:** A company plans to develop a smart home IoT application that controls various devices, such as thermostats, lights, and security cameras.
- **Considerations:** During the design phase, the company considers security as a top priority. They assess potential AI-enhanced cyber threats, such as adversarial attacks and data breaches, and develop a threat model to identify potential vulnerabilities.

### 2. Development Phase:

- **Scenario:** The development team builds the IoT application using secure coding practices and integrates AI algorithms for predictive maintenance and anomaly detection.
- **Considerations:** The team implements security controls, such as encryption, authentication, and access controls, to protect data transmission and device communication. They also perform rigorous testing, including penetration testing and code reviews, to identify and address security vulnerabilities.

### 3. Deployment Phase

- **Scenario:** The IoT application is deployed in a developed ecosystem, with devices connected to a central server hosted in a secure cloud environment.

- **Considerations:** The company follows best practices for secure deployment, including secure configuration of cloud services, network segmentation, and continuous monitoring of device communications for suspicious activities or anomalies.

## 4. Ongoing Maintenance and Updates

- **Scenario:** The company regularly updates the IoT application to address security vulnerabilities and improve performance.
- **Considerations:** The company implements a patch management process to promptly apply security updates and fixes to the IoT application and underlying infrastructure. They also conduct regular security audits and risk assessments to ensure ongoing compliance with security standards and regulations.

## Mitigating AI-Enhanced Cyber Threats

- **Adversarial Training:** The company trains AI models with adversarial examples to enhance their resilience to adversarial attacks and improve their ability to detect anomalies or security breaches.
- **Data Encryption and Authentication:** The company implements strong encryption and authentication mechanisms to protect data transmission between IoT devices and the central server, preventing unauthorized access or tampering.
- **Continuous Monitoring and Detection:** The company deploys AI-powered anomaly detection systems to monitor device communications and identify potential security threats or suspicious activities in real-time.

◆◆◆